The Hypnosis of Life

Self Defense Lessons to Help You Cope With Everyday Pressure

By Roy Masters

THE HYPNOSIS OF LIFE
Previously published under
the title of THE SATAN PRINCIPLE
Copyright © 1988, 1979 by Roy Masters

Published by The Foundation of Human Understanding
Printed in the United States of America

For information, please direct your inquiry to:
The Foundation of Human Understanding
P.O. Box 34036, 8780 Venice Boulevard
Los Angeles, California 90034

or

P.O. Box 811, 111 N.E. Evelyn Street
Grants Pass, Oregon 97526

Cover design: Yuri Teshler
Typography: Jeannette Papp

Library of Congress Catalog Card Number 88-80924
ISBN 0-933900-05-8

Above this race of men stands an immense and tutelary power, which takes upon itself alone to secure their gratifications and to watch over their fate. That power is absolute, minute, regular, provident and mild. It would be like the authority of a parent if, like that authority, its object was to prepare men for manhood; but it seeks, on the contrary, to keep them in perpetual childhood: it is well content that the people should rejoice, provided they think of nothing but rejoicing....It covers the surface of society with a network of small complicated rules, minute and uniform, through which the most original minds and the most energetic characters cannot penetrate, to rise above the crowd....Such a power does not destroy, but it prevents existence; it does not tyrannize, but it compresses, enervates, extinguishes, and stupefies a people, till each nation is reduced to nothing better than a flock of timid and industrial animals of which the government is the shepherd.

Alexis de Tocqueville

A word about Roy Masters

Roy Masters was born in England in 1928. When his father died, he apprenticed as a gem cutter at age fifteen; but his heart was not in being a fourth generation diamond cutter—he was more interested in polishing facets of his own human nature.

Seeing a vaudeville hypnotist on the Brighton stage, he began to wonder, "Why can't hypnotism be used to make people act sensibly rather than foolishly?" Inspired by the idea, he pursued the art of hypnotism until gradually, over the years, he came to the startling conclusion that what was wrong with people was that they were *already hypnotized* by life's pressures, as evidenced by irrational behavior, anxiety and guilt.

Through personal experience and through his practice, Masters realized that the root of the power of negative suggestion lay in wrong emotional response, and so he began to search inwardly for a way to help people overcome the hypnotic power of stress. After years of searching, he found it and called it meditation; he has been teaching it ever since.

His internationally-syndicated daily radio program, "A MOMENT OF TRUTH," is a listener-sponsored, audience-participation show where callers discuss their most intimate problems on an anonymous basis. Drug addiction, adultery, crime, alcoholism, demon possession, the educational system, marital and family strife—all of these may be heard discussed in a frank and meaningful way in the course of a typical week's programs. Roy Masters has appeared as a guest on radio and TV from coast to coast.

As time permits, Masters makes lecture tours of major cities. His "Hypnosis of Life" Seminars vividly demonstrate the hypnotic nature of modern life. He also keeps himself available for public service speaking engagements, and particularly enjoys talking to prison inmates and young people about coping with the subtle problems of life.

Roy Masters' irreverence toward the powers-that-be may account for his popularity with a large and faithful listening audience. His views are always controversial and never fail to evoke listener response, both pro and con.

He has lived in this country since the early 1950's with his wife, Ann; they have five children. He has been the President of the Foundation of Human Understanding in Los Angeles since it was founded in 1961.

Contents

1 The Hypnotic Curse of Culture

The secret knowledge through which the world has been ruled these past eight thousand years has finally surfaced. In the last few centuries numerous attempts were made to prove that hypnotism existed. These were met with swift countermoves to prove that hypnotism was nothing but a hoax. Strange how the scientific community reacted in most unscientific ways! There were fierce outcries and strong censure against certain maverick investigators. Methinks medicine protested too much! It surely must have been some kind of defense, because the phenomenon of hypnotism does exist—it is indeed a scientific fact.

Until recently, the powers-that-be have succeeded in keeping hypnotism quiet. But then such things as the Charles Manson gang, Vietnamese brainwashing techniques and the proliferation of pseudo-religious cults put mind-control in the headlines.

Psychopathic psychics are now crawling out of the woodwork to meet the needs of a fascinated public. Disillusioned with the intellectual, materialistic, scientific approach to human suffering and problem-solving, people are turning away from medical symptom-removal back to removing the *awareness* of symptoms through the occult and psychic phenomena. And, fearful of losing their monopoly of the healing arts, doctors and scientists have begun to stoop to a combination of the occult and medicine. (But our modern witch doctors are really like babes in the woods when they're out of their material/medical element.)

After several hundred years of put-downs, certain maverick medical men have finally jumped on the psychic bandwagon and begun using various forms of hypnosis as a therapeutic tool. They are calling it holistic medicine, by which they mean the treatment of the whole man. They should call it *holocaust* medicine, because the fact is they now have the key to *manipulate* the entire man, mind, body and soul, through the deadly combination of hypnotism and drugs.†

Hypnotism is not—and never was—a therapeutic tool; but neither is it a fraud. Admittedly, hypnotism is a fascinating subject any way you view it. It still is good for a few laughs on the nightclub stage and it can be used to anesthetize some poor fool into having his teeth extracted painlessly; however, these are not its main uses. By employing hypnotism for entertainment and analgesics, you can cover up its much more ominous uses, its dark side. Bear in mind, if you will, that *hypnotism is the instrument of deception, of making the truth seem false and the false seem true so that you can literally cause any effect you desire to bring about.*

---

†Nevertheless, there is a true "holistic" medicine, the real meaning of which will presently be made clear.

The rulers of this world were at first alarmed by the emergence of hypnosis as a bona fide scientific fact. But, seeing an opportunity to turn it to their advantage, they are now busy making what they once labeled quackery into a respectable scientific tool. If hypnotism can be seen in this light, as something to be used in the hands of a competent authority, perhaps the powers-that-be can rest easy for a while.

The Establishment knows full well that the ordinary man in the street is, without his realizing it, already entranced in one way or another. Exposure of the principles of hypnotism strikes fear mostly in the hearts of political, religious, financial and scientific leaders, for it is primarily those "leader" sorts of personalities whose power would be threatened if hypnotic procedures became common knowledge.

Let me illustrate why the mighty are so afraid and skeptical. Suppose that I hypnotized you and then post-hypnotically suggested to your subconscious that you would see as your authority a particular person wearing a red headband† and that you would obey him as you would me. Lo and behold, the moment you opened your eyes that person in the red headband would discover a marvelous power to make you do anything he wanted you to do. And, surprisingly, you would find it your good pleasure to submit to his every whim. That person would have acquired power through post-hypnotic transference.

Now that man with the red headband did nothing for that power, because I gave it to him. But nevertheless, he would have it until I, or someone else with hypnotic

---

† or a Brooks Brothers suit, a stethoscope, a clerical collar, a sergeant's uniform, etc.

power, decided to take it away. Now, "red headband" power is also transferable to other people. In other words, the red headband authority can delegate some or all of his power to others wearing green or orange head-bands if he so chooses, each one of those people having power to transfer authority to others down the line. The person in power could take the form of a political, religious, educational or military leader. But (are you ready for this?) that power is also found in the form of the female, who has inherited a beguiling hypnotic influence over man ever since his fall from grace.

Man, as we know him today, had an origin. Cultures and political systems have origins, too. But suppose the origins of man and of culture were both due to a fall. Then the man fallen into this system will be under its spell, its hypnotic influence—in Biblical language, a curse. "All who *sin* are slaves" to whatever or whoever seduces them away from reason. Hypnotized, we fall asleep to our former way, "awakening" under the system that spirited us there.

No matter how low we sink, we all excuse away what we are as we "awaken" to what we have become. Strangely, the very system or person who made us what we are is the one we elect to love us *as* we are. Our elec-tion of that type is compulsive and slavish. Those people are psychopaths; we, the people, are the psychotics who "use" psychopaths to keep us asleep to our faults.

Somewhere at the beginning of the history of people and "their" systems, there were those who possessed real seductive power, who delegated authority to their own kind. They transferred or passed on this authority to others who dressed, spoke, acted and thought in the ways which would be recognized as acceptable by the hypnotized masses in that system.

Ambitious people (budding psychopaths) are always struggling for this power. But in their ignorance, many educate themselves to behave in the acceptable manner instead of discovering the original secret of power itself. This is the reason why ambitious people prostitute themselves. They are driven to spend their lives studying, struggling to get to the top, to the place where the power can be transferred to them. But, unfortunately for them, *few of those unprincipled eager beavers have any real power of their own*—even when they get there. Little wonder why such (pseudo) authorities, unsteady on their wobbly pedestals, are threatened at the core of their being by the unearthing of the principles by which all sick systems originated.

Please note the difference between culture and true civilization. What we have today is culture, man having fallen away from reality and real civilization. A back-to-front, upside-down social order exists, with seducers as our heroes and gods.

There are two basic methods by which a leader's power can be taken away from him or her:

1) A more perfect psychopath with total knowledge of hypnotism can rise and take the power away from the elected officials of any nation, or

2) A more perfect man, graced with understanding, can simply awaken the masses from their trance state.

Therefore, psychopathic leaders such as politicians, doctors, educators and scientists, fear two kinds of men:

5

those who can put the masses to sleep, and those who can awaken them from the hypnotic curse by the truth, which would make them free.

World leaders are very insecure on their wobbly thrones. A great majority are ambitious fools, emotionally and intellectually drunk on a sense of importance which they have either inherited or gained by being elected. And like the actors they are, they must continually improve their performance to be acceptable to the dreamers who are compelled to elect them. Psychotics (the people) will respond to psychopaths if their inherited brainwashing recognizes the transference in the psychopath's authority and if he makes the right sorts of noises and moves to please their egos.

Those blind leaders of the blind never seem to fully understand the power they have. Like seductive females, their power is gained by default—they have a combination of inherited power and a dash of seductive instinct which shows them how to dress and move. It is a shallow, meaningless existence where learning is only superficial. Do you see what I mean? A "dumb blond" discovers exciting power by simply wiggling her torso. She does not understand her heritage of power. All she need do for gain is to vary her wiggle theme more effectively. "Great" men do not necessarily have to be bright; they need only discover people's weaknesses and "wiggle" for their delight. In this role-playing there is no original power at all; one only need discover weaknesses and play up to them. Dropouts on the ladder of social achievement, be they dope pushers, con artists or cult leaders, work with only bits and pieces of an original seductive theme to keep their followers pacified and obedient for the sake of their sense of power. More highly sophisticated psychopaths scan their victims very carefully, detecting the whole range of needs, desires and weaknesses, before they close in with their scam.

The kind of Svengali personality who originated the system to begin with holds the reins of true knowledge and power; until he returns, leaders are only trusties in a big prison. Remember the two types of people who can take power away: the skillful Svengali hypnotist, and the Christ-like man who has mystical counter-hypnotic knowledge to awaken the people from the hellish power of the serpent of antiquity.

Why is it so imperative for us all to understand hypnotism? Because one way or another it is everyone's trip! All conflicts, subtle confusions, tragedies, illnesses, fears and guilts which we experience are due to a misdirected lifestyle. We all need to understand the mechanism of hypnotism in order to be free from complicated and subtle forms of suggestion.

To solve any problem in yourself, with your family or on the job, you need only understand one principle: how to overcome your ego/emotional response to the pressure of authority—mother, father, teacher, husband, wife, or anyone. If you fail, you will find yourself marrying and electing them to sustain the wrong identity in you. You could never have any problems were it not for the subtle hypnotic power that life in general has upon you to draw you back to the scene of the crime.

The cause of all tragedy is the subtle power of hypnotic suggestion, a subject I intend to explore with you in every one of its diabolical details.

The antidote to hypnotic suggestion is the power of

awareness, which grows out of a state of consciousness (diametrically opposed to the trance state) in which one sees clearly all things as they really are. I have called the practice whereby one comes up to reality, away from the hypnotic dream world of imagination, *meditation.*†

There is a razor's edge that separates hypnosis from true meditation. As they are each practiced they are clearly taken for opposed states of consciousness. However, each can become the other and, furthermore, one can be confused with the other because superficially they do appear to be alike.

It is imperative that we explore these two states of mind, comparing one against the other, so that each can be clearly recognized and understood.

Meditation, is, in a sense, a sort of fixation on God, as hypnotism is a fixation to gods of our election.

Each state has its own teachers leading toward a goal, and each state has a method of getting you there. Allow me to give you a sneak preview of what I mean in microcosm.

Concentration is the way you produce hypnosis; but observation is the way you produce meditation. Observation is the "opposite" of concentration and is the way you free a fixated attention.

If you concentrate hard enough, you will become hypnotized; but if you can observe gently, you will wake up. A continuous process of observing self leads one out of the hypnotic state we all live in towards a source of

†The meditation exercise herein referred to is designed to *increase objectivity,* and is not to be confused with techniques such as transcendental meditation which are designed to relax the user through distraction which promotes oblivion.

knowing called understanding.

Understanding is to meditation as knowledge is to hypnotism.

Worry, or *premeditation*, is the hypnotic counterpart of meditating unceasingly.

Can you see by the little I have told you that there are similar processes going on in each state which produce effects and "answers"? But these answers originate from different sources and the effects are as opposite as good and evil.

Concern is the true caring from a meditative state. Worry is the imposter love coming from the lower realm of mind. Concern heals human relationships, but worry, with its core of self-serving answers, breaks them down. Concern is righteous and corrective, but worry is self-righteous and tempting.

Now there is also an attitude factor in both states: sincerity and insincerity. The insincere cannot meditate; instead, they subvert the meditation instruction and become entangled in hypnosis and personalities.

Your attitude has a polarity which draws the consciousness up or down into different places in your mind. And attitude is also the factor which determines what you believe and what type of leader or lifestyle is acceptable to follow. The wrong attitude (pride) makes the good guys seem like bad guys. It makes the false seem real and the truth seem boring or threatening.

There. I have teased you a little to whet your appetite for what is to come. We shall explore together all that I have said and much, much more.

Every time I discuss hypnosis I will endeavor to quickly compare the parallel processes in meditation and vice versa, so that you, the observer, can see for yourself whether or not you are traveling in the right direction, because seeing for yourself is the essence of the true way.

In meditation, one commits oneself to God's will; but the various forms of hypnotism, if carried to their ultimate conclusion, are meditations to...the devil. There, I said it!

Whenever you dip into your intellect for answers to problems (which you have created through your hypnotic state) your unconscious reaches beyond the borders of your own intellect and without realizing what you are doing, you draw upon a dark, intelligent spirit who suggests an answer in terms of ideas. In the absence of understanding, you believe you thought of it yourself, so naturally you will do it. What has your experience been with such "good ideas"? I mean, does anything ever turn out right? Are you ever happy if it does? I think not! No way! Not for anyone who ever has lived or ever will live.

You see, the spiritual void left by your avoidance of God causes a feeling of great inferiority which pride attempts to overcome with knowledge. And this need to know, this craving, is a signal to a mischievous spirit to attend to your ego needs, seizing upon the opportunity to use your mind as a vessel of his will. You then have a false conscience guiding you, and trouble follows you all your life. And the people who attract you to follow them are a little closer to hell than you are.

Should the answers you receive through this process make you successful, they will also make you a ruthless or a pretentious creature, the embodiment of that invisible, wicked leading spirit. You yourself become a leader, a hypnotist of sorts, who leads others in the wrong direction.

I have explained that culture is not really civilization;

culture is what rises to displace civilization as it falls. The head men of culture, with few exceptions, are psychopaths by nature. Culture is civilization turned upside-down. In this system, most of the people live in reverse. (Perhaps it is only coincidental, but the word "evil" is "live" spelled backward.)

Singular among God's creatures, only man can devolve downward, back through the evolutionary process, away from perfection. The condition that cultural man finds himself subjected to is the result of an original choice or sin. Animals evolve from a point of being less to one of being more, but man moves downward through the evolutionary scale from the point of being originally better. Many degenerate to the point of vegetating. Others mask their bestiality with hypocrisy and frills, compensating for their dying with artificial life-sustaining systems. The entire process is called "progress."

I am not being at all uncharitable when I say that falling men live at the expense of one another whenever they can. It is indeed a dog-eat-dog world. Yet not even the victims of the system are willing to right the wrongs of the culture, for there burns in our egocentric hearts the hope, no matter how faint, that we might someday "make it big" (meaning we might become the one who lords it over everyone else).

It is precisely for this reason that the powers-that-be hold their power; a peculiarity common to all sinners gives it to them. Those who rule come into existence to provide the pattern of our hoped-for glory. It is this particular personal weakness of our egos which leads us to fall as slaves into the system of culture.

In order to better understand the politics of hypnotism,

let us clarify the meaning of some key words. We might begin with the concept of *service*, since that is what our leaders ("public servants") claim to offer us.

I have said that culture is not civilization at all, civilization being of a much higher order. Civilization can come into existence only as the individual consciousness of man is saved, raised up out of the hypnotic trance of sin where it exists as a natural slave of culture. In a culture, it is the people who are the servants (serfs) or slaves, while the leaders (*fuehrers,* in German) help themselves to the people.

Hypnosis is the basis for the curse of politics and policies we fall under and are born under, and the reason for our fallen psychotic/hypnotic condition of slavery is *sin.*

The hypnotic, psychotic accursed state of mind is connected directly to the fall of the soul to the devil ("lived" spelled backward). And most of us do live backward, deluded that it is somehow forward. We continue to "progress" (regress, really) away from reality in order to avoid shame and because there is often a proud stubbornness about preserving the ego-life with its cultural base. Life under any system of culture is preparatory to death, but because we are deluded and live in a hypnotic state, we think it is preparatory to life. To preserve the ego life, we are forced to avoid realizing the truth of what we have become, and that means remaining blissfully in the psychotic state under an ancient curse, while somehow seeing it all as a blessing.

Does it not seem to be a noble thing to be free to do what we want to do, to find others to love us, to make our own laws, to cure sickness and disease, to be a success, to aspire to whatever we want to be and do? "What is so wrong with becoming important and feeling good," we

12

say. The truth is that underneath it all is the ignoble desire to see ourselves as God. In everything we do, we try to preserve and advance the cause of the fallen ego; therefore, the movement away from reality toward any forbidden glory appears as progress in our eyes. But it is not progress, and the only reason we do not see it is that the excitement of our goal blinds us to reality, to the end that our own "reality" might be made to seem more perfect.

Now, every wrong person needs support, upon which is based his sense of rightness; and so each person aspiring to be God appoints someone to serve that secret need. But that person in control of his private life is in turn overshadowed by someone else who is doing it to him. And thus it comes to pass that an entire political system is formed based on families which result from ego-failing and ego-need. The Adams and Eves in that system are bound to exploit the ego-weakness of the others beneath them.

On top of the human garbage pile called culture is the person who embodies most what we all aspire to—the sentinel at the gate of hell. He or she is the guardian and keeper of cultural identity and champion of the faith—the *fuehrer*, president, queen, pope or Indian chief.

Politicians (who *say* they serve) really cater to the weakness of people, and so do all the guileful females who delight in controlling their weak men. Kindly note the vital difference between "serve" and "cater to." True service is a noble thing, but catering is sly and snaky.

Jesus taught that the greatest among us should be the servant of all. True service does not enslave the people. Instead, it brings a divine order to earth—true civilization, in other words.

Serving is a noble act done by noble people. Those who are capable of serving are already endowed with greatness by virtue of their marvelous humility, and they truly serve. The good they do is an outpouring of the good already in them. They do not lie for the sake of power, for the lie is not in them. They already have power—not from the people through election, but from God, to do good for the masses when they are ready. They awaken the people and then minister to an awakened and enlightened populace. Through such men and women the windows of the mind of the world are opened, through which the latent plan of heaven unfolds upon the earth, facilitating the appearance of more and more people with bright natures.

Not so with those who cater to your ego, for their power comes through deception and through people dying to them. Being full of guile, they have no life, no power *except what is gained by deception* to rule you in your dying to them; so they must preserve your falling state. That way, they continue to enlarge their kingdom (of hell) on this earth. Think of it—their good pleasure comes from making you suffer. These psychopaths tell the lies you need to hear, creating problems; then, like angels of light, new variations of psychopaths rise to the occasion of your need to help you solve those very problems.

Each person or group is a king on a mountain, looking down at smaller kings on smaller mountains, seeking the advantage of power and control which comes from putting his fellows on—and down. Catering to the ego is a dangerous form of temptation. Responding to such an ego appeal, you fall into a trance and you find yourself living backward under that problem-solving, problem-

14

causing system of culture. As long as you remain under that spell, your ego can stay secure in the delusion that living backward is going forward. In believing that you are being served, you are really being enslaved, never seeing anything wrong with you or the people who rise to soothe your pain and guilt with their arts and sciences.

There is, then, a politics of hypnosis and a "politics" of meditation, with two different types of men, each led by a different god, attending to the particular need of your soul. The soul of man is capable of projecting and manifesting two diametrically opposed worlds—hell, with all of its sick answers becoming sick cultures and cults, or the one and only plan of heaven on earth.

The ever-presence of God is all around us, yet we do not always see Him. When our egos do sense His presence, His truth is felt as anxiety, fear and guilt, a reality we are too ashamed to face. Escaping, we reach for the security of our culture-hypnotics: friends, pleasure, church, music, drugs, drink. What are we really doing when we are escaping like this? Are we not escaping from the ever-present informing reality, the Truth who is trying to set us free? You see, our vanity does not allow us to be still and know this truth, for then we would become aware of the folly of pride, of what failures we have become at the hands of our lovers, leaders and problem-solvers. And, furthermore, we would be aware of what a hell "our" system is.

Our pride demands glory, not shame—eternal ego-life, not death—and awakening to true knowing takes the hope of these illusions away. But in the presence of temptation, reality retreats, while the false hope which pride craves is present again and again and again. Alas, every hope is more hopeless (but only if it is seen compared with God's reality). Good appears to us as if it were evil, and evil is experienced as good. Very often the fact that we are instruments of some evil thing dawns upon us, but we reject that truth and reach for the comforting lie. Who else will serve us in our falling state, save us from reality and give us false impressions about who we are and about everything being all right? It is the evil in people we embrace, which caters to the evil that is now becoming us.

We are really never in control of anything, but anger makes us think we are. Nor are we being served, as friends would have us believe, but "love" makes us think we are. Rather than face the awful truth of all that, we escape by continually flipping into fantasies of love and hate. In our fantasies we never have to realize how wrong we are, and so the ego way is preserved. We can still play God in our imagination at least, even though the fact is that we are pawns in someone else's hell/dream world.

We are helpless instead of mighty, nothings instead of somethings. We are depressed instead of happy, hopeless instead of hopeful, dying instead of living, because every high from experience becomes the next new low, the power and the reason for the next fantasy.

Behind all of our love/hate relationships is bitterness, and a prevailing fear of God's love. Our bitterness, which came about as the fruit of false love, still craves that same false love to soothe its pain because it still fears truth-love. But sooner or later we must see that our lovers, leaders, poets, educators, scientists and priests cannot deliver what they promised. They lie even as they themselves were lied to; believing the lie, they inherited the power to lead through making others doubt themselves.

To lead, one must accept the lie. As each of us discovers our confusion and guilt, our loss of power and control, we either flip out or we retrieve the power by employing the techniques of deception against other aspiring egos who need us to be their backbone. We draw them away from guilt with promises and dreams we cannot fulfill. In our hunger and weakness, few of us can resist the lure of the exchange—power advantage for a few lies and false reassurance—it is too easy; people are so willing to surrender.

There is no such thing as weak people, only wicked people. And you all DESERVE to suffer at the hands of the tyrants you cling to for relief of your guilt. Indeed, all who sin are slaves, and only the truth will set you free.

Everything which befalls a person emanates ultimately from his own private sin. It is sin which draws the weakling to an amiable rogue who becomes a merciless tyrant by virtue of the temptation such an easy mark presents. Therefore, don't try to save a sinner from his involvement, or you will simply take the place of his tyrant.

If we do not worship God, we shall always be ruled by tyrants, unless the pain of our affliction causes us to cry out: "God, give me understanding. God, give me knowledge of your way."

Evil has a proper role; it must exist in society. There is no way you can root it out, nor should you try. Evil in its proper, lower place serves a useful purpose—we suffer from it until we are awakened by it; then it can be used to bring out and establish virtue in us.

I started out by saying that as civilization falls, culture rises, the tail becomes the head, injustice becomes the way. But in realizing the truth, culture will be converted back to civilization. In civilization, those evil people who were on the top will find themselves on the bottom—tempting the good to become better. And those "lost tribes" once trodden under the feet of the underworld authorities will receive power back—good power—the kind which comes from God, not man.

And then we shall all live happily ever after, awakened under the tutelage of God, no longer asleep in hell.

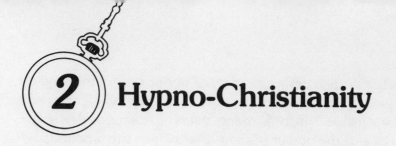

2 Hypno-Christianity

When I was a small boy I became aware that there was something missing in my life, and so I began to search. I asked my parents, my rabbi and my teachers those questions which burn in the heart of every searcher, only to realize that no one had the answers. At least I had discovered one very important truth: no one could tell me what I needed to know. I had to find it for myself.

That brings to mind the amusing, yet meaningful, story about the soldier who went around picking up bits of paper on the parade grounds. He would read each bit and throw it away, muttering to himself, "That's not it." Finally his superiors sent him to a psychiatrist, who gave him his discharge papers, to which the soldier cried triumphantly, "That's it!" You see, he knew what he was looking for all along. In a similar way, every seeker knows in his heart what *isn't* it. That which is saying to him, "That's not it," is really IT all the time. Do you see what I am trying to say?

By the time I was fifteen I had developed a keen interest in hypnosis. At the time, it did seem as though it held a key to the mystery of human behavior. I remember

19

seeing a stage demonstration of hypnosis and thinking to myself, "If people can be made to do silly things, why not the sensible?" It took many years to discover that *hypnosis was the power of folly.* Please give me time to lay a foundation for this statement.

In 1953, about the time the Bridie Murphy publicity was at its height, I jumped on the bandwagon, left my diamond cutting business and opened the Institute of Hypnosis. Before long, I realized that hypnosis was not what people needed—that hypnosis was not therapy (unless, of course, you could use it to lead a person out of that state) *but the very reason people had problems.* Life's pressures were hypnotic and almost everyone was under this influence. Here was the cause of people not being themselves.

Hypnotic influence was the cause of conflicts. Things people did or said under the influence became the basis for their guilts, fears, anxieties and a host of other problems. Victims of hypnotic sins would smoke, drink or whatever, by compulsion, their peer-group pressure being similar to the hypnotic influence that I, too, could induce in my subjects. Quite often, drinking, taking drugs, smoking and other odd habits were attempts by the guilty victims to hypnotize themselves into oblivion. You see, if the tempter-hypnotist-teaser has the power to reduce the awareness enough to make someone sin, then hypnosis is also powerful enough to take awareness away again, this time to remove guilt.

I can't remember just how it all came about, but my own searching resulted in my being led by the Spirit of Reality, the truth greeting my desire to know what was right, even as it can do for you.

Years passed, and changes began to take place in my approach. For seven years I probed and uncovered such secrets as few men have ever known. In the light of those discoveries, my approach to hypnosis began to change into the meditation practice which I am teaching to this day. What I discovered was that I could lead a person out of his lifelong trance, lead him up to a reservoir of knowing (which I later called the light), and at a certain point the subject discovered that the realizations available there had the power to resolve old traumas and give needed direction to his life from within.

I saw the fine line between meditation and hypnosis, where one became the other through a person's rising or falling from grace. Hypnosis was the sinner's practice of losing awareness as a means of solving problems. Meditation, through which the soul sought to *gain* awareness as a means of solving problems, was the reverse of hypnosis. For hypnosis to become meditation, a special attitude was required and that attitude was the love of truth. Those who do not welcome truth are always seeking new hypnotic experiences to escape from reality. The foolish ego finds great relief and comfort in deeper and deeper states of unconsciousness.

I began to see clearly that what was wrong with the entire world was that people were outwardly pressured and motivated. Men were not created to be manipulated by worldly authorities and pressures. We move against our own best interest when we respond to those appeals. People who are in control of other people know that fact. Once we get caught up with their games, we go on responding until that response becomes a conditioning and then we can't prevent them from imposing their will on us. We become fearful, guilty and lost. We can't see how to get back to our own command center and stand on the podium of our own mind to conduct our own life. We even become afraid of waking up because our conscience seems like the enemy. As one lady put it, "I am *afraid* to give up sweets and sugar." Eating kept her secure in her trance.

Once caught up in pressure, the only way we can deal with the guilt of failing is to escape seeing what is happening to us. This brings us to partying, drinking, smoking and other such distractions and pleasures—those things which I have said are self-induced hypnotic states. For while we are yet egocentric, we always deal with our problems by putting aside the consciousness of the problems. This is the way of pride, the way to false righteousness through hypnotic personalities, love affairs, religions, drugs—everything, in fact, labeled "culture." "You set aside the laws of God," said Jesus, *"by your traditions."* The hypnotic sway of culture has the power to make wrong people forget their wrong.

I found another peculiarity of the ego: reality became its enemy after the person was seduced into degrading acts through hypnotic excitements. For until the ego is ready to admit its own faults and make friends with the God of conscience, it relieves boredom and anxiety by using memories of experiences with people, places and things to reintroduce the hypnotic dream-state of oblivion.

I saw how the ego could be tempted by evil and led astray, believing it was on the road to glory; and when the truth dawned the "morning after," there entered a pride factor that didn't want to see it. The soul preferred to stay in its trance.

One plus one made two, and two plus one made three, and slowly but surely, I said, "My God, I see!" And even as I saw, the act of realizing enabled Truth to realize Himself through me and He changed me and my ways.

I saw the secret of the inner way to God. Meditation was the antidote to the hypnosis of the world. The ancient prophets spoke of the light and they also spoke of living in darkness, and here it all was! People preferred the dark theater of their own minds to the light of reality. Down there in their imaginations, they could be what they wanted to be and have what they wanted to have, never seeing what was wrong with what they wanted and what they had become through reaching.

Before I go on, let me explain away so-called hypnotic cures. Suggesting a headache away while the subject is under hypnosis often compels the victim to say that his headache is gone, even when it is not. The subject must dramatize the hypnotist's will as best he can. A person under hypnosis reflects the will of the authority post-hypnotically. Suggest that the subject had been in Florida, wake him and ask, "Where were you last week?" and he will reply that he was in Miami and fabricate other details—the bars he was in, all the girls he met, and so on. His mind makes it all up as he goes along, amplifying and rationalizing what he was commanded to accept. But there *is* a certain state of consciousness (which I later understood to be meditation, which brings the soul back to reality) that can be responsible for really curing headaches. Sometimes a hypnotic subject will trip into the meditation state by chance. Most hypnotherapists do not realize that real cures under hypnosis do not come from hypnosis at all but from a state of induced reality. I found that two states of mind existed, separated by a razor's edge. Hypnosis, induced a certain way, could sometimes become a meditation by "accident."

Another interesting thing and a very curious fact to me was that I found that only certain people (are you ready for this?)—people who were believing Christians—could be cured permanently. This was a very puzzling actuality. I had to find out what it meant. Here I was, somehow having the power to lead people to reality and right there at the gate was some kind of magic principle that I, the therapist, the guide, didn't yet understand. Those people had a part of the mystery and I had the other part. Together we had a whole.

Sick Christians who came to me simply weren't Christian enough. If they had been Christian all the way through, they would not have needed the services of a hypnotist. But many were searching people of "Christian" hypnotic persuasion; that is to say, they had practiced a surface Christianity through pressure and conditioning, contrary to the way Christ Himself taught.

I would speak to them about my discoveries, about responding to pressure and ego, about love and patience as a defense against evil hypnotic pressures called temptation, and about bringing them to the stillness of their own souls to realize reality. They would even exclaim, "That's all in the Bible!" And I would say, "Oh really?" Later I would consult the Bible and there it was, almost word for word—the very thing I was teaching. Somehow I was grasping it deeply, understanding it deeply, and to some degree practicing it, while they were not. They were acting out verses and chapters which their souls agreed with, but one vital ingredient was missing: the intimate contact with the light, the ability to respond to it directly rather than being carried along and away by the preaching of mere words. The difference is between knowing all about the sun and yet never feeling its warmth. Wordy descriptions do not allow one to grow as the real experience does.

So that is how it came to pass that I became interested in the Scriptures. I found that I was speaking the Bible to people, having never read it myself.

Another extraordinary thing is that I could also help Jewish people (who were not the dogmatic, dyed-in-the-wool, saved-by-the-law Jews) if they were searching persons who were open-minded and seeking answers. It seemed that those who were helped the most were the ones who lived within a moral framework. The truth leading me was also leading me to the truth in them. We were actually helping one another. Strangely, I had the power to get people to realize the truth deeply enough to accept God intimately, *but only those who could eventually accept Christ as redeemer ever remained well permanently.* Prior to their experience with me, their faith in Christ had been superficial; that is, they weren't able to have a true faith. All they had was an intellectual knowing.

We can, of course, know intellectually and yet not be able to know it so deeply that it saves us. "Lord, I believe, but help my unbelief" is a line from the Scriptures. You see, I could help a number of people by suggesting a better way of life, which in turn tended toward freeing them from the grasp of certain vices. In effect they were waking up. However, as some of them awakened they became afraid of the truth. For they were not yet ready to give up their pride. And they stopped meditating.

As a matter of record here, I do not wish to push the

Messiah on you, knowing that it may merely reinforce the "ameners" among you who are already hypnotically caught up with the church. I know, too, how many people have rebelled against hideous "Christian" pressure. But given time, with the key of meditation, many rebellious or "non-religious" people can come back to a moral framework and appreciate the profound wisdom of the Bible.

The problem with most preachers is that they are not credible. Let us say your son is reported killed in a train wreck but somehow, deep down, you know he is alive. A "friend," trying to comfort you, tells you, "Oh, he is all right." Although this is what you want to believe, you cannot accept it because the messenger is only trying to comfort you with the truth—he isn't credible. But what relief the believable messenger brings! That seemed to be the same kind of experience I was bringing to the people I was helping. If they were truly searching, I could awaken them to the truth, my way being so completely believable that they could be saved from the hypnotic grasp of the world. Since that time I have called my meditation Judeo-Christian.

I neglected to say that the unbelievable messenger of Christ pressures you with his message, so that if you knuckle under you conform not to the truth, but to the wicked spirit behind his beautiful words. And if you rebel he follows you, amplifying the guilt of your resentment and rejection of Christ, driving you to drink and drugs and waiting to catch you in his hellish trap on the way back.

All of these revelations led me to my own persuasion about Christ, because the more I taught and meditated and the more I applied to myself what I was applying to others in bringing them to the light, the closer I myself came to it. So in teaching people I found myself learning from them, and in their learning from me I was also learning from my own self. And so it came to pass that I slowly realized the profundity of the Holy Scriptures.

There unfolded before my eyes the truth about man's fall and the plan of salvation from the fall, the hope of which burns in the hearts of all seekers. The reason why we feel so hopeless is because we have been confounded about salvation by the very words which might have saved us. And as far as the rest of the heathen, scientific, atheist world is concerned—for the most part they don't even know they are fallen beings. They still vainly believe they are evolving up to some kind of glorious future. They can't even see how they are all working toward personal and global disaster.

Prideful mankind solves problems by medical means, by psychological means and by other compensatory arts and sciences. The worldly wise fail to realize that all problems come from falling (failing) and from trying to eliminate the symptoms of it. Not realizing that this is the case, and being hypnotized by their belief in the power of science to cure them (you see, that way they don't have to change), they continue to place their faith in the very spirit that caused the downfall of man at the beginning. Misguided belief—hypnotic belief—is what leads, guilt by guilt, anxiety by anxiety, to the gates of death and hell. For instance, if you believe in evolution, how can you be saved? If you believe that you are the product of progress rather than a fallen being, there is no need for salvation. The relief you feel, and the freedom you mistakenly think you have, come from believing the lie and reaching toward the forbidden, away from the pain of realizing you are wrong. That is addiction, whether it is addiction to an idea, to the foolish hope of a cure, or even to religion. Addiction is the evidence of ego stubbornness. The choice is between what is killing you and what could wake you up to reality.

Slowly but surely I began to see that belief in what was true was a tickle point, a magic touchstone. I saw that people were always believing in and even wanting to believe in wrong—compulsively.

It is most difficult to tell a person the truth in his fallen, subjective state. Lost in that dream state, he cannot receive it properly. Information mixes in with all of his learned errors and prejudices so that he can't realize deeply and clearly. A person tends to cling hypnotically to religious words as though they were the reality, and there is some kind of relief in that because they seem to mean salvation. But I found a different kind of agreement with the student who was in the meditative state. He could see the truth, not only because I said it, but because he, too, could see it for himself; he could believe and act from the *realization* rather than from suggestion.

If I were to preach to you about Christ, Moses and their philosophies, at best the words would just mix into your brain with all of the prejudices and knowledge you have already gathered there, and become poisoned. Words scramble together in your mind and come out in rather strange combinations, usually excusing everything that is wrong with you.

For example, see how easy it is to believe that your problems come from worldly suggestions and from pressure. But just knowing that isolated fact can increase your conflict, because you can use that true knowledge to blame the world rather than look at your own weakness, which allows suggestions and pressures to affect you thusly. Not feeling right about being "right" can drive you to study the word of God even more compulsively. Or that same inquietude can make you rebel and go to pot, as if that were the more honest way. And indeed it would seem to be, for religion practiced upside down, with the earth as the reference point, has the earth spirit. An evil nature tends to enlarge in you under a veneer of holy verses and chapters.

I also began to see that in order to believe truly, you have to be motivated by what you realize, what you have found to be so and believe for yourself. You can listen to Roy Masters or any other teacher 'til kingdom come (and it won't), accepting good principles by rote memory as one way of placating truth. For many people, the rote word with its ego-expanding qualities is preferable to an intimate experience with God. That is believing, but it is definitely not the kind of self-realized and self-actuated intimate belief which saves. That lesser kind of belief, even when it concerns Christ or any sound principle, can be lethal. Belief cannot save you unless it is *self-realized belief*. Flesh and blood must not reveal it to you, but my Father in heaven. Devilish preachers, knowing this fact, rob you of this vital belief-experience by feeding you too much knowledge too soon. At this point you become guilty for believing you are saved when you are not. You also pick up the wrong "holy" spirit from your preacher and the wrong in you becomes addicted to hearing the word. If you miss church one Sunday, you feel the same guilt and terror as does a drug addict who needs a fix.

Here, I found, was the deep mystical reason why some

people would recover from the most horrible diseases while others, subject to the same therapy, even the same teaching, did not. Many professing Christians were threatened by the idea that they were not yet truly Christian. Since this was the truth about them, their prideful egos naturally rejected it, for they were the kind who used religion to justify all their wrongs. Their egos were guilty, afraid of giving up the hypnosis of religion and truly facing the reality of Christ. This group, paying lip service to Christ, could never hope to recover from sin and sickness. But when the seeking people came up to the light, they were grateful and became reconciled with the Spirit of their conscience. And so, in believing and receiving the truth and light deeply, they experienced the touch of God. They were able to experience repentance and through repentance they were saved from the power of the world and healed of all manner of terrible afflictions.

Briefly, that is the story of how I arrived at the Judeo-Christian meditation. Naturally, there will always be those to accuse me of being a devil or an Antichrist. If I am against anything, it is hypocrisy. There will always be those fools who wish to remain hypnotically caught up in verses and chapters as an escape, and who use Christianity (or any good thing God made) to confuse others.

Christians in name only are very, very zealous about their "Christian" faith. Their guilt makes them hypnotically rigid, lost (as if saved) in this rigidity. What they really have is churchianity. Their church-directed hypnotic state programs them to act like Christians. Repeating the nice words of the Savior, they are caught up in those ideas which produce a religious chatter and an illusion of salvation, perpetuated by rituals that post-hypnotically reinforce what the hypno-preachers have established. They know *about* the Son, but their growing guilt makes them afraid of *meeting* Him in person, and consequently they have to work harder at lighting candles and rubbing beads, to chase away the evil spirit of conscience.

Any idea you get caught up in—whether it is Jesus Christ or (forgive me) spaghetti and meatballs—is an *idea*, a hypnotic fixation, that can introduce a new guilt at the very moment it takes your old guilt away. What it saves you from is conscience. Notice the two types of salvation, the two ways of being innocent and justified "by the blood." The foolish ego is saved from guilt by another temptation, while the wise soul is saved from temptation so that he is no longer answering to the world. Any noise or excitement can do it—even truth. Music can produce that same bliss, the relief being so great that you feel a thankfulness, a gratitude like a religious feeling toward the musician-savior. Any excitement, pleasant or unpleasant, can do the trick. Even something to hate can be used to make you forget your own guilt.

Christians who are not really Christian all the way through have become self-righteous and self-satisfied. Afraid of losing that "faith" and falling again beyond redemption, they cling to the deception of their salvation. Such as these see my words as a terrible threat. To take away the veil of deception, which to them is a refuge, would bring them back to honest guilt. They would burn in the light of heaven as if they were in some kind of hell.

Now another thing. It is easy to cause any person (love object) to love you by thinking love thoughts toward "it." It is easier to do this if "it" loves you first. We all live with love and hate, for we need the excitement of both for relief of guilt. We misread or misunderstand what people say and we get upset. Later, the guilt we feel compels us to reverse that process in favor of love. So be careful of the "Christ" who loves you AS YOU ARE and thus makes you forget guilt. Be careful about pulling that stunt on others. You know the old line, "God loves us first and saves us by that love, so must we love others with His love." That hypnotic trick of instantly accepting people is a trick of the devil, a misuse of the real meaning of love.

Every wicked charlatan who ever walked the earth preached that God loves you *for the fallen ego state, not from* it. The devil's masterpiece of rhetoric is that "Jesus loves you" as you are now. This bait is so exciting to your ego that you are easily caught up with what is supposed to represent Christ, just as you get inextricably lost in any appeal to your ego. Then that which sets you up compels you to forever accept it for continued favor, or else you will start to feel the damnation that was there all along. You are not saved, but fooled.

Some of these are "Jesus freaks," others fundamentalists and some "charismatic Christians." All are really hypnotized zombies. Although they act out Christian roles, they could just as easily be hypnotized into fancying themselves Napoleons. Christians such as these are very guilty human beings indeed, because in using Christ in this wrong way, a greater guilt accrues to them, along with a greater need to escape by post-hypnotically fondling melodies, crosses, verses and chapters. Churchianity is the religion of escape into images and sounds and not an embrace of reality—as Christianity should be.

Two different spirits wait on man as he comes into this world, and the inclination of the soul is the invitation to either the spirit of knowledge or the spirit of truth.

Let me elaborate by comparing knowledge with understanding. The best way I know to spark understanding is through the spoken word, and the closest I can get to that in print is to transcribe one of my impromptu lectures on the subject. It is presented to you here in the hope that the spirit behind it dances across the words and awakens your soul from its lifelong sleep. Let me warn you—these words mean business. They are going to wake you up, whether you like it or not. So you had better not listen if you don't want to realize the truth.

Let me show you what I mean by truth. Now there are two sides to knowledge: there are facts, and there is the recognition of facts as fact.

> One plus one equals two, does it not? Now I ask you, "How do you know that is so?" And you might reply, "My teacher told me." Surely that is not a good enough answer. Now if you ask me how I know that one plus one equals two, I shall reply, "Because I can see that it is so." The reason I can say this is because there is an inner testimony to the fact by the truth which made it a mathematical fact.

Let me elaborate. Now the inner testimony to the fact, that which reveals the fact to the observer, is the truth. The fact itself is not the truth. Although the fact is true, it is only a manifestation of the truth which made it a scientific fact. *The Truth is the Spirit who made all facts true.*

Now the evidence that truth exists is that we can recognize fact. That part of you, that part of the self which testifies to you, the observer, that one plus one is two—that is the truth. And that is the Spirit who has formed this particular immutable mathematical principle. The Law-maker testifies to His own law; taking that one step farther, the Creator also testifies to the creation, even as the created fact itself (all His creation) testifies to a Creator.

Your parent spirit, the Creator of the universe, is within you, and all facts to you must be evidence of His presence. To know in this way is understanding.

Now each of us has a code (whether moral or not) of living, and if yours is moral, you will entertain moral thoughts. In the process of dramatizing them, the pattern of that code will become facts in your life—a witness to others of the Truth who was there from the foundation of the world, expressing Himself through your person, just as He is doing through me now. Just as the Truth testifies on behalf of His own created fact, so does He also testify against what is not true. With such ever-present knowing, you are safe.

Therefore, I speak to you with wisdom, not merely quoting you facts.

If you are perceptive, you can see when a man is simply repeating what he has heard like a parrot, not really understanding what he himself is saying, yet feeling very holy by spouting knowledge. You can tell where such people are coming from.

Listen for yourself. See if you can hear that I am speaking to you from the Presence in the moment, not preparing a thought or a word. The truth in me collates memorized facts, and when I speak to your soul inspired by the spirit of understanding, you know in your heart that I am not speaking from a rehearsed text, or merely rearranging what others have said before me. You know deeply that these words come to you moved by the Holy Spirit.

So you see, there are actually two qualities in one: there is fact, and there is understanding of the fact, which is very much alive, collating facts to have meaning. That is why there is LIFE in the words I speak to you. For these words seem to speak to you from within.

Do you understand now what Jesus meant when He said, "My words are life..."?

Talking to your soul about this delicate thing should be too marvelous for words, because if you stand in awe of what these words are saying, you are blessed to understand and to perceive.

You have both kinds of truth. You hear and understand; you see and perceive, and the spirit dances across the words and awakens you to truth with fact, and by truth to fact.

Facts themselves, devoid of spirit, acquired for an ego sense of importance, deaden you to reality. They have no life-giving, awakening qualities. Yet misguided people specialize in true facts, and when they preach they distort them to rationalize wrong lives. By speaking facts to you, not having in themselves the spirit of understanding to awaken you with those facts, they can hypnotize you with knowledge and deliver you to the spirit of knowledge in this world.

Because knowledge alone is lopsided and neurotic, the spirit of evil, which seduced man from understanding at the very beginning, is able to operate through it.

There is a very profound and basic principle here. The first recorded act of man was to fall through knowledge of good and evil. On the other side, he left behind the truth of truths (understanding), which humbles man and makes him realize and stand in awe. Compensating, he moved away from awe, wonder and worship toward the gathering of facts in the hope of becoming God through them. So that when the seducer speaks to you to this very day about acquiring knowledge, you look up to him because he represents what your ego wants to realize about itself. You admire other knowledgeable rogues because your own ego needs them to pattern itself after. Therefore, knowledge from them is acceptable and inspiring.

The same is true even with religion. One can feel very pious indeed losing oneself in one hypnotic religious experience after another, since they are accompanied by inpourings of religious words and concepts but are without true testimony. The only testimony that you have in this condition is a swelling up of pride and a growing feeling of your own "greatness." But feelings deceive you. You can't see that because you won't see it; there is no understanding to expose deception. Your ego will have rejected understanding in favor of puffing up in knowledge. The real religious experience comes from being caught back up into understanding.

I know sweet and gentle Mexican peasants who can barely read English who love to hear my radio program. Yet many intellectual giants accuse me of double talk, only because they are threatened by my understanding.

The faithless live in worlds of proof. The kind of belief produced by empirical evidence cannot save you, but faith can. First, though, you must know what faith is.

I once had a partner in business and we were talking one day about the shape of things to come—the handwriting on the wall, the political storm clouds gathering on the horizon, and so on. When I mentioned something about putting some food aside and some means of protection, he suddenly puffed up and said, "God protects me."

The big arrogant fool looked at me as though I were some kind of sinner for lacking faith in God's power to protect. He happened to be a self-righteous knowledge-collector who was a student of mine—the kind who goes from one guru to another and then comes back to save you. But with all that knowledge, he did not have understanding. Not the way I do (thank God).

Do you know what I replied to him? I said, "When you see rain clouds gathering on the horizon, then you know enough to take your raincoat or umbrella. The ability to see ahead is the understanding that nudges me to put food aside and to provide some means of protection for my family. That is the most fundamental form of God's protection. The fact that I can see ahead is the gift of the Spirit. God gives me the understanding to realize danger and to prepare to meet it. If you are looking for some other magic power, my friend, forget it. It does not exist. Higher forms of protection and understanding beyond that point may exist, but not for you. You must follow understanding to Understanding, if you see what I mean." God does not grant the power to perform miracles to those who have no respect for the simple tool of perception which he provides for us first.

The ability to see clearly is understanding, and that is, in part, God's protection. Understanding IS that protection: to know about things so that you say "yes" instead of "no" or "no" instead of "yes," to make right turnings instead of left ones. Understanding is a knowing without always knowing why you know. But you do know. When you do not doubt that knowing and you follow it, that is faith which bears fruit in fact. Wisdom, insight or intuition born of common sense, is life. Furthermore, it cannot be gleaned from external sources. When understanding comes, knowledge ceases. You must not study truth. You must not cram the knowledge of God in your head. The very Scripture you study tells you that the letter *killeth*, but the spirit giveth life.

What does that mean? It means simply that anything intellectual, including verse and chapter, regardless of how true it is, consists only of second-hand *facts*—facts which are supposed to awaken the soul, not to teach it. Get that through your thick skull—YOU ARE NOT MEANT TO LEARN VERSE AND CHAPTER. Study kills. It is a very dangerous "informing" indeed.

Any kind of study can kill you! Beware of too much knowledge too soon. Words program your mind and rob you of the life which comes from realizing for yourself.

The letter kills. The words themselves are dry bones, dust. But the understanding of it, the spirit behind the words, gives meaning and life. Those who thump the Bible, preaching and hollering the word at you until you are reeling in agony or ecstasy, tempt you to reject God by such pressure-learning. Through your objections to them, they make it appear as though you were rejecting God's truth. You are not—but you are caught in a terrible trap, damned if you do and damned if you don't, until someone with understanding comes along and says, "Hey, it's okay. By all means read Scriptures, but do not study. Do not commit knowledge to memory by effort of will, even if it seems you must fail. You are not going to fail or go to hell if you don't study. You are more likely to fail and go to hell if you DO."

To repeat, the Bible you study tells you, "The letter killeth, but the Spirit (of understanding) giveth life." So now, when you read a passage in the Scripture, it is good if you naturally recall what it says. I am not going to argue with that. But don't stuff it in your ears. Don't let psychopathic teachers pressure-instruct it into your mind.

For Christ's sake, don't let people "Jesus Christ" you to death.

Don't let those wicked fiends lay that kind of trip on you. Furthermore, don't let them bamboozle you with half-truths like "Jesus loves you (as you are)." That is intellectualized truth—rhetoric, really. Evil, taking holy names and words in vain, often appears as a ministering angel of God, an angel of light. Feeding you with love-lies, evil nurtures what it has created in you.

Understand how this world is being destroyed by distortions of fact. Without true understanding, you cannot see what they are doing to your mind. I know that all of you who have been seeking, who are God's very own, who are destined to come to Him, knew this all along, but you lost the witness which is appearing in you now. The sheer force of everyone being carried along in the world made you doubt the witness in yourself.

So don't doubt yourself anymore. Be free now in your mind about these things. Certainly the ever-present God loves you, but only through repentance—for doubting the witness (understanding) and accepting the word of the world (knowledge)—can He love you *from* what you are.

3 The Psychology of Hypnosis

All dyed-in-the-wool psychotics have a need to be dominated and, conversely, psychopaths have a need to dominate. Psychotics feel insecure and fearful when they are not dominated, while their counterparts, the psychopaths, panic when they are alone without someone to control. Which one are you?

The more guilty he is, the greater is the psychotic's need for a more powerful, more dominant psychopath to "free" him from anxiety. The need for the more dominant personality grows steadily in direct proportion to the psychotic sleepwalker's guilt. However, the psychotic is

41

rarely conscious of his need to be dominated. He perceives any ruling personality as his servant—a court jester perhaps—one with charm and entertainment value to make the psychotic "king" feel good about himself so that he does not have to face the truth.

Although truth is omnipresent, we are tuned out in the way we might tune out one radio signal in preference to another. The signal of the station we are not receiving is nevertheless all around the radio set, though not coming through our receiver. The ego can avoid ever-present reality only by living in the imagination (the psychotic-hypnotic state of mind), which exists in relationship to an external source—the hypnotic pressure-personality or psychopath. *If you do not love reality, you will require the services of a hypnotist (and hypnotists come in many guises) to pull you away from it.*

The psychopathic personality has earthly power, not the power of honesty; he has the kind of power derived from keeping you feeling secure. Power personalities don't live in a dream world the way you do; they don't have to—they are successful, and your fear and falling assure that. Their success appears only in contrast to your failure (but you keep serving them anyway in the vain hope that the qualities you so admire in them might evolve in you).

Now please remember that your soul or consciousness is incapable of originating thought, just as a radio set cannot originate its own programs. Therefore, as your soul comes down away from reality, it falls away from a plan or a "program" which is waiting to come through. You then pick up the other program, which originates in you-know-where. In time, you unconsciously take on all the characteristics and the nature of that source. Belief in the lie joins you, tunes you in, as it were, to the source of deception.

Every soul which has fallen to pride is void of understanding, because the ego shuns knowledge of God in order to be God; the ego fears understanding because that is the way of God. Understanding shames and inhibits the way the budding ego wants to believe about itself—egotists want to will their own universe into existence and to reveal their own creative genius so as to be admired for their accomplishments.

The fallen ego is hungry and thirsty—not for truth, but to realize its own greatness, which somehow seems to elude it. When we have lost sight of the truth, we often misconstrue the guilt we feel for this. Check this out the next time you feel guilty—you can falsely believe that you are guilty only for not being good enough, rather than for being wrong. Guilt then drives you to do better to prove that your goodness is there. Manipulators can use this folly to make you serve their purposes; often they can be responsible for making you feel guilty, and then allow you to work it out by serving them in exchange for a smile of approval.

The tempter helps us dream the impossible dream and then, no matter how low we sink, he is there again in one form or another recognizing our worth, adoring us, catering to us, worshipping us, understanding our needs and sympathizing with our suffering, even helping us to restore our pride and self-esteem.

We fall prey to such ego appeals all too easily. Falling always seems (at the time) like rising; escaping reality has exactly the same effect. Then, the morning after the night before, we see what has happened—but again, we cannot handle what we see. We cope with the awareness of it by flipping back into a hypnotic/psychotic state, talking down to our tormentors in our heads (we are afraid to oppose them in reality because what enslaves us we also need for our continued security). We construe our enslavement to psychopathic masters to be a sign of goodness, and we see ourselves as unselfish martyrs, hoping that eventually our unfailing service will make them recognize our kingly worth.

In this system, you find yourself subject to the authorities who have risen in the fall of man. The master-slave relationship inherited from your parents is perpetuated throughout your life by people you meet, elect and marry. The spirit of that which made you what you are loves you as you are.

Like a moth to flame, you are drawn into relationships (it is especially noticeable in marriage) unconsciously selected to reinforce the loser role you have been cast in during your formative years. A small stretch of the imagination will help you to realize that a similar reinforcement process is going on in the "winner" too. Cowards make bullies, and bullies make cowards; they reinforce one another's roles, you see. The coward is actually responsible for contributing to the power the bully has over him; that power comes from the coward's very own weakness. Such lack of courage is rooted in fear, and fear comes from a lack of faith. The cause of fear, metaphysically speaking, is the loss of confidence in what is right; courage comes from knowing and believing the truth, and being committed to what is right for each moment, rather than from being popular. But the fallen ego has come down to the system of believing in itself through the approval of others. There is no way you can oppose the evil you inherently *need* to support your ego, so you tend to find security in that evil.

The degree of fear and inferiority you experience in response to authority is in direct proportion to your distance from reality. And that, in turn, is directly connected to your own special brand of ego-tripping.

I repeat, everyone on an ego trip (and therefore wrong) is dependent upon support from someone or something; playing God demands approval—some call it love. To feel right when you are wrong requires deception; in order to be deceived, you must have a *desire* to be deceived. The desire to be deceived, when fulfilled, makes you comfortable in the presence of the deceiver, and in that moment you become guilty.

Love, as we know it, is actually an ego-hypnotic need. Excited and overcome by any form of recognition, the ego is enticed down to accept the offering, away from painful, boring reality (in other words, it sins). The next trauma occurs when we experience the relief (escape from awareness of the last sin) which love-excitement brings, plus again getting the bonus of believing that we are wonderful.

The psychopath's power grows as he teases his victim into a dream of omnipotent ecstasy, and he can do it either with love-offerings or with hate-offerings. Let me elaborate.

In its imitation of God, the victim ego is both king and judge, flourishing and growing on either extreme of love or hate. Being loved and loving the lover is the king ego-trip. The judgment side is exercised when someone provides you with a hate-offering by treating you unkindly. You can be made to feel very superior indeed to the wicked person who triggers your judgment.

Thus, psychopaths can be twice as effective through being cruel one moment and affectionate the next. The psychopath who initiates the love/hate responses is the tempter, gaining power by reason of the victim's fall. Temptation is the cause, and response is the effect. And by making you respond, the effect for them is power.

The effect of response for *you* is a high (which is really a failing). But, while responding to temptation causes your ego to swell with pride, it also throws you into internal confusion and conflict with God, whose position you have usurped. Therefore, guilt is formed, driving you to need more love from the teaser in order to forget the guilt and psychological confusion caused by the last encounter; you become addicted to being loved in order to assuage the guilt of being loved. Mysteriously, you cling, yielding power to wickedness as it gives you approval.

You will do anything to get that love; you will give yourself, your identity, your very soul for approval. Once you begin, you cannot stop. The more wrong your ego becomes, the more you need reassurance that you are not wrong, and all that demands more lie-love which leads to more guilt, more craving for love and yielding to hypnotic intrigue, which then sets you up to hate. If you are rejected, you tend to fulfill yourself with hate and judgment; if you are accepted, you eventually become miserable and hateful too.

The craving for love is like a vital need for life, and it is—the life of the failing ego. However, to escape one psychopath, you must attach yourself to another who, by helping you feel good about yourself again, makes you need him in a worse way. All your energies are siphoned off by the people who provide for false ego-security by entertaining you with the love/hate experience. And you tend to be very protective toward those people, groups, systems, corporations or whatever—you rally around them as if you were defending your own honor.

Those who lie-love you in this fashion rob you of the life of your own root sytem within by displacing your true God-self, and slowly but surely they smother the life out of the real you with false concern for your false well-being. No one is ever as obliging as he appears to be, for you must pay the piper for the security of your pride with compulsory service. Servitude (loyalty, in your eyes) feeds the wickedness of the system under which you exist and encourages it to reward your weakness with a brownie button, as if that weakness were virtue. So what starts out to be a friend, loving you and catering to you, one day emerges as what it was all along—a fiend, taking advantages. When they appear as fiends, they have "value," too—you can then use their wickedness to feed the need of your king-ego to know itself as God through judgment.

Your private dictator is not free either, because he becomes dependent upon your servitude and addicted to dredging up from hell fiendish ways to tease you with love and hate to sustain him in his parasitic existence.

Like all ego-tripping psychotic dreamers, you find yourself cast in the role of loser, which forces your guilty ego to cling to emotional love/hate experiences in order to avoid awakening to the awful truth about yourself. The truth is: you are not good and wonderful as you like to think; you are instead a weak, sniveling, treacherous coward—a slave in someone's private hell. You love evil's love and you love to hate it, too. Both your love and your hate give it power to become meaner, to provide judgment food for you to live on in your fantasy.

To hold on to your self-righteous, pathetic security, you must cling to your hypnotic illusions. Strangely enough, the basis of all false security lies in being corrupted and in being a coward, in bringing out and cultivating the worst in others so as to have your weakness hailed as virtue. You must see all failings as virtues in order for your security not to be threatened. You can't help feeding the worst in others because that is the treadmill all weak-minded sinners are on.

Therefore, in your sin-state you must go on giving power to overbearing personalities to shock and traumatize your system with cruelty or with mind-bending love.

Perhaps your terrible need for love will eventually create a fear of the "love" experience. Then you may try being indiscrete, getting your lovers to be cruel to you so as to experience the contrast of relief which comes from love's opposite—hate.

Everyone you love, you hate; and everyone you hate, you also love (need). And every one of these shocks to your system—traumas—has the "marvelous" effect of throwing you into a new hypnotic state which helps you to forget the guilt of the last episode.

Look at some combinations: you hate your lovers because you sense that they are somehow responsible for your unhappiness. Again, you hate them because you sense that your need has made you a slave of their love, so you are not free as "God" is supposed to be.

You also secretly hate your lovers because you have

made them so cocksure, so swelled up with conceit and power that they take liberties with you. But you can't speak up and so correct what is wrong with them because you need the presence of wrong to provide you with judgment food for the relief of guilt and for pride. You may be able to smile while you resent them secretly, because by smiling you conceal your real feelings, approving of that ugly thing your weakness has brought out in them so that you can enjoy luxuriating in hate. What you feel toward them (resentment) gives you pleasure by distraction. The pleasure is judgment of others, which helps you forget the judgment on yourself, and that is what makes you smile with false happiness. Judgment puffs you up, it makes you feel superior to your dictator; even though he is lording it over you, you feel better than his wickedness by comparison. Sinners, you see, always live by comparing themselves with others.

For this basic reason, the downtrodden tolerate their enslavement and their enslavers. In such a system, neither side is to be trusted—both are treacherous beyond belief.

Think of it—a world where people elect and cling to those who corrupt them, for imagined security. Eventually, people give evil so much power that they are destroyed by the very evil they embrace. When evil lie-loves, we cling; and when it becomes cruel, we find pleasure there, too. The resentment we feel is like sweet candy. We can't give up resentment because it provides the excitement we need for the relief we need; it is the energy required to keep us in a trance, lost in our mental wonderland as king and judge.

Notice what happens as you try to give up resentment.

See if you don't experience the pain of self-denial, feeling as if you were giving up life itself. For lo and behold, if you do not have anything to gripe about, you will feel unbearable loneliness and guilt. You will feel as though you had lost all the virtues and goodness you thought you had. Resentment gives us a sense of our own strength and importance. Not having a hate-offering threatens the bastion of ego-security because it is hating wrong which makes us feel right.

Most people have a diversified portfolio of escape tactics. When simple resentment will no longer suffice, you can escape into worry the same way you do into images of the people who trouble and traumatize you. Trouble with people leads to problems in life, and you react to those problems which have come through your reduced awareness with people in the same way that you react to people. The escape into the problem is called worry. Worry creates more problems to *react* to, which then provide the fantasy basis for more worry.

You escape into these "problem-traumas" just as you escape into traumas caused by people, and you come to need problems the same way you need people who trouble you and help throw you into a trance. Think of it—not only are you drawn to people who destroy you, but you also unconsciously *create* the problems with which you are burdened.

Each succeeding mess in your life is indirectly connected to the person who set you up to fail; that is why your resentment toward the problem, which is designed to help you escape from seeing your failing with people, actually forms a chain of memories leading back to them. So, when you can run no longer, you remember with

50

bitterness and blame all the way back to those who originally set you on the path of failure.

In this manner, what you thought you buried through people-experience and problem-experience comes alive again at the end of your journey to hell.

To summarize: when our lives begin with cruel traumas, then guilt grows up because of our resentment (supporting our judgment); this drives us to seek love to soothe the pain, and thus we become involved again with wickedness. Whoever loves you in your wrong is the dominant wrong, who lies and promises what he cannot deliver in order to get what he wants. You cling to him for the security of the lie-love. Remember the rule: you cannot be attracted to or affected by deception unless your ego loves (needs) deception for its continuance.

Evil serves us in our dreams and keeps us in our dreams, but in reality we are its slaves. Life is full of betrayals, cruelties and tragedies which always come by way of our seeking for sick love/hate ego-support.

As I have pointed out, the psychotic is just as dangerous as the psychopath, because he is the creator of wickedness—the quiet submissive one who *spoils* people into taking liberties. If you are not already a psychopathic taker, the subtle treachery of the psychotics is liable to draw hell up in you to serve them lies. They spoil with super-sweet submission, not the kind of service which gives *them* any power, but the kind which gives *you* their power to take advantage, to excite them with love/hate rewards.

Psychotic mothers change their children into cripples, or mad, rebellious, fiendish criminals through their doting, weak submission. Psychotics set you up to make demands so that they can secretly hate and feel superior to you, both by servitude (their apparent goodness toward you) and by the judgment against the demands they have tempted you to make. Servitude is the only way they can realize their own goodness. When this process is carried to extremes, they can make you a vegetable. Many a "good wife" has totally destroyed her husband through year after year of such relentless service, reducing him finally to a decrepit, incontinent, barely ambulatory infant-tyrant.

Correcting these spiteful, treacherous, yet innocent-looking psychotic sleepwalkers is not easy; in fact, it is well-nigh impossible, for correction is the farthest thing from their spineless souls. And if you give correction, they usually twist it to their secret use. Between loving and hating you, they use you for an almost perfect illusion of their own goodness. Believe me, most of them deserve the vampires who will prey on them until they die.

When they are devoid of the desire for truth, there is nothing anyone can do to set them free. Such people cannot tolerate freedom from tyranny because freedom means facing truth and shame. They love the slavery which seems like freedom with great honor. *Therefore, be warned about being a leader-type trying to help people who follow and hang on to you for advice.*

People with no roots in themselves and no hope of salvation may *tempt* you to correct them. To put it another way, they tempt you to tempt them by "nagging" the good into them. You may begin by good-naturedly pointing things out, which effects an apparent repentance and gratefulness, favoring your ego. If you accept honor or what appears to be success, you will feel the guilt and responsibility for them as they falter and that will cause you to rise to comfort them in their suffering. The guilt you feel, as well as the load of responsibility, comes from being tempted to tempt.

This is the way psychotics solve their problems of sin and guilt, while corrupting the goodness of the innocent. So, while they may seem to be sorry, they suffer not from repentance but from being found out. And if they cry, it is because they are angry children trying to make you have pity on them through their tears.

When your greater perception makes these weasels conscious of the shameful game they are playing and of the plight they are in, they may condescend to let themselves be guided by your wisdom. That is to say, they latch on and benefit by your words and parrot your lifestyle without having to recognize reality and experience meaningful change. By using you the way they use their corrupters, they can pull you into their heads and fantasy with your image, remaining self-righteously secure in a trance.

Pretending to want understanding (knowledge, so as to look good in the eyes of others), they respond to correction in very strange ways. Expose a motive, catch them in some ungracious act, and they will appear very sorry, grateful for your pointing it out to them. They may seem to have really been awakened and helped, as though correction had actually taken place.

But guess what. They never are really sorry; they are sorry only for being found out, and their feelings of unhappiness and sadness exist for the same reason. They had conferred upon you the power to direct them, not to expose them, so when you do, they feel they have the right to resent you. It is a cat and mouse game. They may learn to avoid each particular sin for which they were corrected (in front of you, they will). But sooner or later they will be guilty of another indescretion, showing that your correction did not take. The likes of these are neither honest nor self-policing people. They use you as a hypnotic reinforcement point to keep them in an omnipotent state of judgment. Later on, they may come to see your goodness as the sign of a devil-manipulator, and their evil as God.

Meanwhile, as slaves of your "correction," their lives continue to deteriorate; with their families, they use the knowledge gained from you to excuse their actions, and then they secretly blame you for what goes wrong. In other words, they love you for the benefit of false righteousness and then blame you for their own weakness in being caught up with you, so they never have to face anything wrong with themselves.

Using you secretly, they not only escape reality but they often succeed in exchanging identities with you and leading people astray with that stolen identity. In all temptation relationships the evil projects into the person tempted so that he appears to be the guilty party, the cruel one who is doing the manipulating. A good man can thus appear to be an evil Svengali with dangerous hypnotic power.

I must admit, it is difficult to relate to psychotics unless you become a psychopath yourself. As I said, they need you to aggravate and upset them in order to function. If you treat them like human beings, most of them feel threatened, and will not recognize your honesty and fairness. They may try to deal with your "threat" by simply not doing their best, unconsciously trying to force you to be upset with them.

54

Usually, they betray you by forgetting little graces or promises, or they employ some petty form of neglect you cannot put your finger on. And other times, just when you think you have them, they will hand you a perfectly logical excuse which you cannot really disprove, and which could well be true, except that you know secretly deep in your heart that it isn't. Eureka! Can that secret knowing make you resentful toward them!

My car mechanic is such a man. He always leaves little things to fix next time around. He does excellent work and is very conscientious about saving my money. But when I complain about the little game he seems to be playing to aggravate me, he has the perfect excuse: he claims that he is fixing more important things for my safety. I know that he is hiding temptation behind that excuse, trying to aggravate me to be upset with him. But what can I say to prove it? I know deep down what he is doing to my mind, even though he himself is not willing to be conscious of it. Under cover of being concerned for me, he tries to upset me, to make me become mean, demanding and unreasonable like other people. Then he could get the energy to function and to escape a psychotic feeling of inferiority to me, which my (honest) presence enhances. For instance—he was supposed to get a door handle for my car. It took one year, and I reminded him seventy-five times! You see, after it became apparent to him that I was not going to provide him with the motivation he needed to do it by getting upset with him, he rebelled against getting it at all. He finally gave me one with the wrong color free of charge and that was the end of the matter. (I should have pushed it all the way, though.)

As I said before, psychotics have subtle ways of trapping you into being an object of love and hate. To give you another example, I once helped a young man establish himself in a business and I also gave him my trade. Not wishing to take advantage of my friendship, I would insist on paying him a fair price for his work. Never—not one time—did anything work out well. Shoes were ordered in the wrong size, belts were made too small. Other jobs were short on quality. He always tried to make it good, though; he was always polite, fair and willing to charge less for what was not up-to-par.

For years I watched and puzzled over this and, without making judgments, as time went by I began to see what he was doing. Unconsciously, he was constantly trying to tempt me to be angry, to make demands and pressure him. Without that kind of stress, he could not function for me personally. In order for him to do as well by me as he did others, I had to be made to fall from grace and become like them; otherwise, I did not have the hell-nature that could be served for the approval he needed. Because I gave him the opportunity to act out of the goodness of his heart willingly, it eventually became apparent that there was no goodness there. This natural failing (you see it even in your kids) tends to evoke wrath and pressure. By upsetting you they justify themselves, judge you, and see their servitude as goodness, making up for the guilt of their own anger by placating yours.

Such people need someone for motivation and some-one to blame. The mechanic is now his own boss, having inherited a business from a negative, psychotic/psycho-pathic partnership. What will probably happen next is that he will do to all of his customers what he did to me, in one form or another, until they start getting mad at him. But chances are they may not show it outwardly, simply because good mechanics are hard to find and, besides, he always has a good excuse to cover himself that his customers find hard to counter, making them doubt what they see. If they don't get mad at this mechanic, he will be unconsciously compelled to make more obvious mistakes to anger them. Or, he could become super-obliging in order to tempt them to take advantage of him. Then some customers, feeling frustrated and not knowing why, will shop for a new mechanic or else they will become so demanding that they upset him into telling them to go elsewhere. Guilt then will drive him to do more and more for them, for less and less. End of business!

Conversely, when a psychopath is in business, he charges too much (sometimes giving good service as a bait to hold the customers till he gets them conditioned to pay higher and higher prices). His extreme greed eventually creates a revolution among his workers and customers. Most businesses fail because of just such personality defects.

The psychotic doesn't handle responsibility well. He is unable to take the pressure of the work load alone because while he needs pressure to work, he also needs someone to blame when things fail to work out right; for that security, he needs to be mothered by a dominant personality. It is rare for a psychotic to handle his own business; he tends to hand over all the responsibility to a psychopathic boss or wife. By handing over responsibility, he is able to function fairly well for approval, but if things go wrong, he blames his boss, partner or wife so he never has to own up to any weakness. It's the perfect security—or is it? The psychopath gets him in the end.

Like children, psychotics realize their "goodness" only by way of pressure. Without it, they are inhibited, paralyzed by anxiety and guilt. The syndrome is self-perpetuating because such paralysis draws criticism, which becomes the pressure needed to forget reality, providing the imprint and the motivation to evolve, to compete, and to compensate.

Without pressure, the psychotic's inferiority is revealed; he forgets guilt, fear and inferiority through pressure. His giving in to demands is not seen as weakness; rather, it appears to be an unselfish giving of himself...the persistent kindness of a god toward his sometimes thankless and undeserving subjects. This type of "good" never overcomes evil; it actually nurtures and *preserves* wickedness to provide contrast and motivation for its own growth. We always draw to us cruel, thankless exploiters and leaders who become the basis from which we develop.

Resentment is the basis of such weak "goodness." Resentment's first pleasure is in judgment, which produces guilt. Through guilt comes false sorrow, misery, and lastly surrender to the tyrant (false compassion) to receive another ego-illusion of goodness.

In submitting to dominant personalities, the psychotic finds both motivation and image-reinforcement. Psychotics are cowards who rarely stand up to their tyrants openly, because they are careful to preserve (through surrender) all that lovely rottenness they need to reinforce that particular identity in them. Ironically, they worship their corrupter because the corrupter represents the god that they are hoping to become.

Therefore, never try to save anyone from his tyrant unless you want him to cling to and love/hate you too. Psychotics enslave themselves to you, just as they did to the last tyrant they love-hated, by putting you on a pedestal and making you a new hero to worship (thus making themselves king-makers, greater than the elected king). In their serving you, you will be serving up to them part of your (wicked) self. See how the stars of stage and screen get torn to pieces by an admiring crowd of people, all of them hungry for a piece of the greatness of their heroes and gods. You hold power only to the degree that you progressively lie-love or ravage with cruelty.

If you are naive—not tending toward willful psychopathy—then psychotics may temporarily benefit from your good advice. They won't really appreciate you, though, because they won't be able to see where their "benefit" is coming from. Few hypnotized persons are aware of the external source of their development. In general, egotists tend to believe that any benefit originates with them. When things go well, they are very happy in your presence, giving you power to keep them "innocent," shocked and programmed with the image that rubs off from you. But when things go wrong, or when your presence weakens, you bore them. They resent what seems to be your love's failing (failing to maintain their illusions). After making you feel your failure to love them, they promptly dethrone you and appoint another hero or lover to take your place— quite a common thing in marriage and other close friendships or fellowships.

The funny quirk about psychotics is that they love and respond to cruelty and pushiness because then the identity they need for motivation comes across in the exchange.

But now suppose you don't play the game, and persist in responding only with patience and graciousness so they are eventually exposed to themselves. Then if it is in them to repent, they are grateful. If not, the pain of being exposed makes you seem like the bad guy to them anyway; they become horribly resentful toward you in a way that cannot work in their favor, but rather works to awaken and break down their psychotic sleep.

The presence of innocence as a pressure-source has a peculiar effect upon the stubborn psychotic mind. The very truth they are trying to forget becomes imprinted in their minds through their resentful resistance. Resentment, you see, is used to forget reality and to reinforce the false identity through judgment. Your innocence simply reverses the process; the spirit behind patient love comes into them through their resentment and conflicts with the purpose of resentment. I assure you, it is sheer agony.

There is nothing more painful to the dyed-in-the-wool psychopath or psychotic than to lose power or to be awakened by the Spirit shining through another's innocence. Psychopaths panic! Psychotics are shocked into a dream world, but with a new imprint or message that tends to war with the spirit of pride and makes them want to jump clean out of their skin. Innocence, you see, represents the very truth that they are trying to escape from (into their minds). Psychotics—try it out for size, if you must. If you must become angry with these words, you will bring into your mental world the very reality you are trying hardest to reject. To hate without a real cause makes the emotion of forgetfulness become the emotion for remembrance. The average psychotic is in no immediate danger of being related to innocently, however, because he keeps himself so carefully surrounded and hemmed in by tyrants.

I'm sure you have experienced the aggravation of having to take your car back to the garage dozens of times in order to get satisfaction. To be sure, the average psychopathic serviceman has no intention of fixing your problem. He not only expects you to throw in the towel and give him your money without his having to work for it, but he also gets a kick out of upsetting the life out of you in the process—throwing you into a psychotic dream-state for the comfort which *you need* to escape seeing your failing to deal with him. Governments gain power in the same way. People hate paying higher and higher taxes, but they give in at the end, giving power to the system to be more wicked. If they didn't have a demanding government to trouble them all the time, they would be miserable indeed. Look at the divine justice: the sinner views his own enslavement as freedom, death as life. No psychotic (sinner) can ever set himself free, because he maintains he *is* free and righteous. While using the exciting presence of all the psychopaths he loves and hates, he gives them the ultimate power of the punishment of death.

Remember what I said about the psychotic's need to be dominated as being a compulsion to be enslaved. "All who sin are slaves," says the Good Book. Happily, there is an escape clause provided for those who truly wish to find another way to live: "You shall know the truth, and the truth shall set you free."

You ought not to waste life's valuable moments reacting to temptation. If you are tempted to take advantage of those who take advantage of you, and if they tempt you to tempt them, in one way or another you will

61

become like them—addicted to taking advantage and to being taken advantage of. You will never, never be free until you bear trial and loss calmly and graciously. If you maintain good composure and meet stress with dignity, you will grow from every encounter. If you should lose money or property—even family—you will still benefit from every temptation in terms of character growth.

True freedom and real success come through meeting temptation with grace. Bearing loss and injustice without becoming bitter makes you better, forging the character out of which good things eventually grow. It is through giving up the desire to get even, which is fueled by resentment, that we may eventually find our way out of the hypnotic system. Until we wish to rise above our lower nature, we will forever be locked together as psychopaths and psychotics, instead of living together in harmony with reality as free human beings.

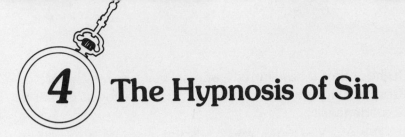

4) The Hypnosis of Sin

Another way of expressing the idea of a psychotic's need for domination is in terms of the NEED TO BE CORRUPTED. All psychotics live and have their false sense of well-being through continually being corrupted. Their sense of becoming and of selfhood depends upon being degraded. (Indeed, there are numerous "holiday camps" springing up all over England and Europe which fulfill the need of the psychotic to be degraded.) Tempted to indulge in judgment, either through hating or "loving" a dominant personality, the victim gets a high on the shock or trauma. The psychopath, on the other hand, revels in corrupting and controlling his victims through being the love/hate object (this is the basic principle behind brainwashing).

The first trauma one experiences induces an altered state of consciousness accompanied by physical changes. Each succeeding mental high produces a new physical low and the awareness of these symptoms of failing is felt as self-consciousness. Guilt is experienced as a result of observing the physical changes induced by the ego's (the observer's) failing. The ego has become less for aspiring to be more; it has sinned† and so has become separated from reality, stained and caught up in a lowly growing-experience.

The shock or trauma that pulls the ego away from reality provides, for a fleeting moment, a delusion of grandeur. Under cover of the thought process, an engram (a sort of memory) is introduced, around which a sensuous nature develops in a devolutionary fashion. The psychotic victim then becomes *addicted* to gathering his identity through traumatic experiences with people while he gathers the natural (compensatory) substance of his being from pleasure. You see, his substance is based on a *lie*.

Temptation separates man from the internal, spiritual root-system, so that afterward he can no longer grow in a proper spiritual way. He becomes addicted to pleasure objects and to shocks at the considerate hands of the tempter. The need to be corrupted translates into a craving for pleasurable experiences, selfish goal-fulfillment and material things.

Ordinary, everyday objects have symbolic, hypnotic power to suggest. A gun suggests power, revenge, selfhood. Money suggests importance. Fine clothes suggest beauty to the wearer. Just as we identify with people, so can we also identify with objects having symbolic values that suggest to us qualities, virtues and powers missing in ourselves. By acquiring and surrounding ourselves with such objects, losing ourselves in beauty, and by believing in beauty, it is possible to become oblivious to the ugliness

†You should understand that the definition of *sin* is not limited to a list of obviously immoral activities. Sin is the inevitable result of a prideful attitude, and it is expressed in as many subtle and varied ways as the perverted imagination of man can devise.

and horrors in ourselves and in the world. We may even come to think that everything is perfect (including us, of course).

Politicians and manipulators are quick to recognize the latent motivating and suggestive powers of material things. They use this knowledge for their benefit by holding high objects which promise power, superiority and glory. By egging us on, politicians keep the people pacified, grateful and controlled through stimulating the need to acquire objects, at the same time erasing any awareness of *their* control over the masses. Alas, the people are forced to pay higher and higher prices to their ruling psychopaths to be released from the guilt of having and being had, to have and to hold more and more.

The root-system of trauma has two vital life-support functions:

1) every new shock helps one forget the guilt of the last trauma;
2) at the same time, it generates the need for the substance of pleasure.

Two needs, one growing from the other, draw the psychotic sinner to dominant psychopaths for their inherent power to help create in him a glorious identity as he selfishly grabs all the gusto he can from experience.

Psychotics fear and resent awakening to what is really happening to them. Their guilt, which catches up with them in the absence of a psychopathic pressure-presence, is misinterpreted as being guilt which is appearing for the first time because of not being good enough. Their failure in life is turned around and construed to mean simply that they have not received adequate recognition. The psychotic remedy always consists of one variation or another on the same faulty theme: they work harder to acquire objects and please people, often giving up ill-gotten gains to their masters in order to assuage guilt and for approval. And then there are always those new traumatic adventures with dominant personalities that whet the appetite again for things.

Psychopaths delight in teasing their victims into being rooted in their hypnotic personalities. Where hate is not employed, "kindness" (false love or spoiling) is used to corrupt, confuse and keep the victim off balance to prevent him from reaching within himself for true answers.

Corruption, entering in through spoiling love, cries out to the parent spirit for reinforcing love. The reinforcement which produces forgetfulness and support for the false identity, comes by way of a traumatic love or hate experience; either one, or both, will do the job very nicely. Those who have been violated through violence feel "loved" and reassured in the presence of cruelty. For example, people who have been held hostage and subjected alternately to violence and fits of "kindness" by terrorists or kidnappers, feel loyal to their captors and can rarely be made to testify against them.

The corrupter never answers the problem of another ego with correction (throwing the person back on his own inner self), but rather with false assurance or with cruel pressure, either of which reinforces the wrong and develops the victim's dependency.

To be saved from sin and death, you must become objective to sin, and at that point you will become subject to reality (saved). But no egotist can tolerate responsibility to what is greater than himself, and so he needs the services of evil to spirit his soul away from its responsibility and its inferiority to God the Reality. Lo and behold, he no longer lives objectively, subject to God. Instead, he is deceptively objective, never realizing his subjectivity to the "servant," evil. *To serve is to rule.*

Involved with his deceitful servant, the psychotic thinks he is above everything and beneath nothing. It is the duty of the resident psychopath to preserve his sense of glory and growth. Gone is the truth, which could tell the slave that he is free only from good, committed to evil for the delusion of glory and freedom.

For this reason, the psychotic masses have little tolerance for freedom from their psychopaths. We all cling to them like kids with teddy bears, to keep us secure from reality. When we, the people, are encouraged to purchase our various pleasures, we do not realize that we are really selling ourselves into slavery.

We are all really dying when, through the use of people and objects, we think we are living. Always, *knowing the truth about our morbid condition appears to be the failing itself.* It is like waking up to discover that our house is on fire and, being content to believe that awakening had caused the fire, going back to sleep as a way of putting it out.

Only awakening from the hypnotic sleep of sin can save you from escaping one psychopath by means of another. Barring that, each false salvation you experience must be at the hand of someone more weird, more bizarre, more wicked, more powerful than the previous psychopath. The last comfort, at the hand of the angel of death, can seem as if it were the spirit of truth come to take you to your haven of rest.

Like moths to a flame, we are drawn magnetically into

trouble, tragedy and danger, for even they can represent life, liberty and the evolution of ego-selfhood. "We have to have problems," we cry. "Where would we be without challenges? We don't want things to be perfect—we need challenges to grow." Ah, but the significant difference between the children of darkness and the children of light saying this is the *manner* in which they grow from stress.

The morally weak psychotic responds to stress, capitulates, and then hides in sleep. In his trance, he conjoins with the evil behind the sleep-pressure. Then his failings are soothed, accepted and rewarded by the psychopath as though they were virtues. There is only one way for the seducer's ego to grow; he must be the one who provides challenges, traumas and seduction, and who finally consumes the substance of his unwary prey.

The seducer, then, is always one step ahead of his victim in terms of cunning—he has a certain kind of sly perception functioning that allows him to make the first moves, which are always calculated to provoke response.

Psychotics, on the other hand, are always reacting to *everything*—even the problems which they create. Every little or big mistake which comes about through their diminishing awareness is like a surprise—another nasty shock which moves them further away from reality. They can even learn to react to tragedy so as to "benefit" (psychotically) from the experience, to justify themselves the way only egotists can. Reacting, you remember, excites a man's soul into a trance state of forgetfulness and omnipotent self-righteousness so he never has to see his sin. It is almost like becoming innocent.

The sinner does try to avoid realizing the horror of what is happening to him, no matter what; but when he cannot, he blames and resents the trouble that befalls him (especially when it is his own fault). When he discovers that tragedy seems to be more under his control than success, and that it is also useful for escape, he becomes accident-prone, delighting in and producing a variety of misfortunes for a "poor me" ego-trip. The stress of suffering produces a psychotic dream-state that relieves guilt and makes the victim feel absolved. "I certainly didn't do anything to deserve this," he tells himself innocently. The psychotic "innocence" produced by suffering is mistaken for suffering for righteousness' sake. So he becomes a martyr, but he never sees that his punishment is self-inflicted, and well-deserved. Thus, even through failing, the psychotic sinner can find false innocence. But whether it is through the trauma of ambitiously achieved "success" or the trauma of failure, he always gets to play God, glorying either in success or in judgment for being hard-done-by.

Guilt can drive rich people to poverty and failing people to success (and sometimes back again to failing). Or, they get hung up with the agony and ecstasy of success and cannot stop being successful; the same can be true of the psychosis of poverty and failure. (You know—thinking it to be the will of God, taking comfort from squalor and priding ourselves in nobly making the best of it.)

The need for pressure can cause us to attach ourselves to things we cannot afford, to spend our money on useless objects (more sources of aggravation) until we are financially backed against a wall or a deadline. That pressure then turns us on and makes us "come alive." Pressure is always needed to awaken the sensuous nature and to provide motivation—the drive to work and live or be—so that we can preserve our illusion of goodness.

Just as you surrender to people through pressure, submitting meekly to their will for the delusion of being superman, so do you do the same with things and places. Unfortunately, finding comfort in an object or place for security, you tend to *become* whatever it is, and whatever it is becomes you. You can feel that what happens to it happens to you—someone dents the fender of your car and you feel as if he had broken your leg.

> Hitler became Germany and Germany became Hitler.

> You are the job and the job is you; losing your job is like losing your life.

Because work upsets, excites and tempts, psychotics often *become* their work; they are lost in it, fixated, loving and hating it in order to function. Most of them cannot think outside what they do, nor can they go beyond what they have learned traumatically. They are often disabled from doing anything else because, without the love/hate work-presence, they become insecure and afraid.

> You can become your house and the house can become you. Through extreme guilt, you may even feel the house drawing you into its walls.

Newspaper headlines capsulize stories about stubborn old fools who die in their burning homes rather than leave them because without their houses they are nothing. Old people often identify with that which makes them secure—their homes, their mates and their money. Upon the loss of businesses, wives, houses, or other material possessions, many prefer to end it all to be with whatever has gone rather than realize what they have become in their downward journey through attaching to things and people. When all else fails, death is the last comfort!

Attaching and escaping, the more you need, the more you will need. Letting go and seeking, the less you need, the less you will need. As a seeker, you become more distant from things; you can own without being possessed. But as an escape artist, you lose yourself in the things you have acquired, absorbing, as it were, all the symbolic values. But when people possess you through your need of them, then you come to a turning point in your relationship with *objects*. You no longer absorb them; they begin to absorb *you* by the way you cling to them to escape the grasp of the psychopaths (to whom you used to cling in the same way).

Some women allow their bodies to be abused in order to get the money to buy a new dress, fur coat or diamonds. Here is the principle of compensating for the real value one has lost (virtue) with the ego-adorning beauty of acquired objects.

Remember what I said earlier about the growing need for objects of escape and illusions of grandeur which results from sin and trauma. For example, if a man can't get to be upset with his wife, he also cannot enjoy his drink; in like manner, we will take terrible abuse from our bosses so as to enjoy more fully the relief of "unwinding" at home. As I said before, we actually *look* for things to upset and traumatize us:

1) because we need the hypnotic escape value, and
2) because the pain of emptiness and loss awakens the sensual nature and *generates* the

craving, the "right" to grow egotistically and compensate in pleasure.

Psychotic egocentrics place little value on virtue, happily trading it all for a mess of pottage. Giving up virtue creates the *lust* for life and pleasure (and later the pain) they need to feel, which they think of as *love* of life.

A prideful and thus selfish person can only get his substance by something around him breaking down. On the one hand, he needs to be corrupted so that the prideful identity can continue to be soothed; and on the other hand, the implanted, reinforced identity grows to feed on the ectoplasm of substance released by his destructive use of people and things around him. A social chain gang is thus formed, wherein every corrupter is also a victim, giving up his substance, but also corrupting others and taking their life.

Corruption, whereby the prideful identity is introduced, sets up insatiable hungers for things in the world. When these hungers are temporarily satisfied, the substances cling and give form to the identity of the corrupted soul; so appears a living ghoul, sucking up earthy life only to be later drained of that life for the sake of identity reinforcement.

Reaction and overreaction can be an "adventure" whereby you lose yourself in any exciting experience. This phenomenon is what we refer to when we speak about "sensitive" people. Sensitivity to life is really a weakness which conveys to the victim a sense of virtue about everything that is wrong with him, including the sensitivity itself.

Adventuring into food, music, drugs and other experiences isolates you from the ugly world and from your own ugliness in newly-developing compartments of your mind, freeing you from the awareness of guilt and despair. Then there are sexual traumas. In fact, you can plunder just about anything to produce the effect of growth and life—freedom from guilt and fear.

The excitement of a speeding car enhances the sense of life for the soul. Parachuting through the sky can produce a sense of life, too. Even inanimate objects can be empowered to provide needed trauma. Don't think for one moment that you have no control over the process—you do, but only when you are *willing to wake up* and face reality.

In paranoia, the victim projects the feeling of being watched from within (guilt) to being followed from without. He reads meaning—intrigue—into external experience to help him transfer the inside to the outside through reactions. The odd thing about paranoia is that the victim is likely to choose a relatively innocent person for his "persecutor" rather than one who might be really guilty of it. The psychotic-paranoid personality, unable to handle the more powerful love/hate psychopaths who originally introduced the guilt-ridden sin identity, finds comfort by creating his own, less threatening pressure-source. Guilt causes feelings of persecution, but if he can seem to be persecuted at the hands of people other than those who made him guilty, he can be freed from being reminded of his part in it.

False innocence comes in from outer reference points, as guilt does through pressure. The shock of being persecuted or accused unfairly can impart a sense of innocence to even the most ignoble of people. The "defendant" gets the trauma he needs as the basis for his judgment, plus the bonus of feeling innocent in his self-righteousness.

Remember the rule: inherent in all trauma is the principle of exchange, whereby the servant becomes the master and the master the servant. Loaded with guilt and feeling old age and death creeping up on them, parents can become their children by reacting to them and making them react back. They can take on their children's youth, identity and behavior patterns while the children become saddled with the responsibilities of irresponsible parents who act like kids. Children take on parental guilt and become old before their time, enervated and debilitated in a bizarre exchange. In a similar way, we can take on the relative innocence of the people we accuse and judge.

Locked into a personality, we react in order to grow more perfectly in the likeness of the corrupter. Often that is the only life we know, having lost sight of our original innocence through the trauma of sin. And we are under a compulsion to serve, to give our all—our life, riches, honor and power—to psychopaths because, having become a loser, the only way we can become anything else is to become them. To lose the corrupting presence of a parent or a friend is often the same as dying with them; to fall from their grace is to experience guilt, and so we rush out to marry a reassuring mother in a wife or husband.

Since hard-core psychopaths fear losing power, while psychotics fear awakening, they all join forces to vanquish the truth. Both victim and tempter are at war with reality, the victim deluded that he is God, and the adversary contemptuously knowing he is God (having the real power). Their common enemy (conscience) is easy to conquest— they merely lose themselves more perfectly in one another in good times and in tragedy. They both falsely triumph over what seems to be an external evil, which is nothing more than conscience trying to "get them."

Primitive natives conceal themselves behind hideous masks to keep away from what they think are evil spirits. Guess who the evil spirit is—the Holy Spirit of truth, which reveals what decadent, despicable, degenerate maniacs they have become.

Modern church rituals embody more highly sophisticated "evil-chasing" traditions. Special ceremonies containing poetic, post-hypnotic triggers help dispel fear, despair and guilt, giving back to the sinner the illusion of hope and faith. Rituals and traditions, devised by psychopathic priestcraft, are the equivalent of the incantations of witch doctors in primitive tribes. Nevertheless, it still boils down to the fact that we need phony ministers to bring us the good news of false faith and false hope in a false salvation attributed to a false god, whose love makes us feel good so we don't have to wake up and change. Sensing something wrong, the devotee may attempt to give up his hypnotic religious practices, only to feel the terrifying presence of the "evil" (good, really, in the form of the pain of conscience) from which he was escaping.

For centuries, man has been led away from Truth with truth (words, rituals and symbols). Truth is something we have always known and never practiced. Should we awaken, the Holy Spirit could whisper the wordless message to draw us away from sin and closer to Him. But in our psychosis, we take religious words, memories, experiences and images into our dream reality. We put the truth on stage and make it entertain us with religious excitement, producing a psychotic sleep in which being saved from seeing our guilt becomes "the salvation of the

Lord." The engineers of this kind of religion are the devil's own psychopaths.

Mixing emotional response with religious suggestions such as love, salvation, forgiveness, Jesus Christ and the blood of the Lamb, subverts the true purpose of Holy Writ (which is meant to awaken and lead one to higher awareness) by using it for programming and hypnotic escape. In this perversion of the promise of salvation, the truth seems to set one free, but in reality it is again another freedom *from* God, to *be* God. Here, closeness with hell can feel just like closeness with God, a salvation from the "hell" of heaven.

Over the centuries, the psychopath has gotten his rapacious claws on religion and used it to persecute non-believers as though they were witches. These "witches" were, for the most part, decent people who could see through the mad psychopathic concept of psychotic religion for the masses. Under the hypnotic direction of these psychopathic priests, psychotic zombies slaughtered millions in the name of God, thinking they were doing Him a favor. The psychotic zombie is the vessel through which hell's work on earth is manifest. Yes, in our selfishness, we are all responsible for the tragic human condition. Thinking that we do our own thing, we all end up manifesting evil's purpose. *We are, in fact, in charge of one another's destruction.*

Don't let it ever be said that I am against Christianity, religion or education. Don't ever let anybody make you think that, and God forbid you *dare* think that about me yourself. If what I have said has threatened your world, I suggest you have built upon a very shaky foundation. And if you resent learning the truth about it, you will be putting a curse upon yourself. In hating the truth, you will be hating God in you, and so you will be doomed (unless you realize, of course, what you are doing wrong). I have the authority to say such a thing to you because it is a true fact. And if you don't believe me, try resenting these awakening words for a season.

When you hate him who speaks the truth, who is moved by the Spirit, you show how much you also hate the same Spirit Himself. If you were one of those Christians who truly love God, you would not hate anyone because hate could not be found in you.

It is the serpent in you who is recoiling, shrinking from these words of truth because the good in you is being set free.

In the past, you have been moved away from reality within you towards the realm of intellect with words, and part of you has become worldly. You needed to hear worldly words to sustain your ego in its fallen intellectual state. And here you have stumbled across the shining light of truth, like a conscience on the other side of your intellect, representing the very spirit you have been running from into sensuality, into the spoken word and the written word. Here is the truth, homing in through the medium of the written word, awakening you, tearing down the refuge and barricades of your intellect.

It is doing something to your mind, coming in through the back door and the front door. I must say, it is not mere words doing it to you. Words are awakening you, pricking the bubble of your delusions, smashing down your mental idols from within and without. You may think it is a person following you around, causing the conflict you feel. The conflict may come by way of me and my words, but it is not from me, the person, but from the Spirit I awaken in you. Conflict comes from your resentment against the Spirit that is in me, the person, which Spirit is in you too. Resentment towards any person will set up anxiety, but if you are upset *with these words,* your agony will be especially excruciating. And if you will not acquiesce to the truth, this battle will kill you in the end, as sure as I am speaking to you now in word and in spirit. Your own hatred, your own rejection of the spirit of understanding, can destroy you from inside. First, though, you have a warning and that warning is the pain of anxiety.

You are not reading ordinary words. But neither are you reading the word of God. You are reading the words FROM Him. The word of God is a testimony in your heart to the fact of the word from Him.

These words are bringing back into your world the missing quality of understanding, the leavening that leavens the whole lump. I may have more in me than you do, but thank God you have enough in you to recognize what I am saying, enough to cause you to turn around and repent of your sins and to reject the dead letter of the law, for the spirit of the new. And these words are a testimony to that fact, a testimony that is easy to accept, not like the hellfire preachers or charismatic God-pushers.

No, you will not be damned if you have rejected religion, because what you have rejected is not religion. And you won't fail if you can't learn. For study is not really learning. You have not failed; you have almost succeeded. Surely, if these words were written by an invisible man it would seem as though you knew me intimately. I am your true spiritual brother, and it is our spiritual Father who testifies to that fact in you.

Worldly authorities are dangerous; they are not true authorities. They play with your mind. The intellectual, emotional preacher has two messages coming out of him; he is saying two things at once. By using Godly words, he pressures you to accept a bad spirit behind those words. A terrible confusion results because you can sense that. You feel tremendous pressure to accept God, Christ and salvation as he presents Him, and because you don't know how to handle it, you rebel or conform. But you find yourself in trouble either way.

People who masquerade as men of God have great force. But they have no power against the truth which is awakened in us. Lies cannot prevail in the light of understanding.

The new life, the way to reality, comes not by listening to people saying, "this is the way," or "that is the way," even if they are telling you the truth. The way is by a private realization of such things—those which can be said and those which cannot. For the new life cannot come from following someone else's wisdom, but it comes from understanding in the moment. If you give outer authorities the power to direct you (the way your conscience should), you will be simply following hypnotic suggestions again. The hypocritical way of the world will still be your way.

No one can follow the truth of words unless he also follows the spirit that is behind the words. Remember, words can lead with truth away from Truth.

Careful how you listen to any words of wisdom, for just as they can awaken, they can also send you into a religious trance, a stupor in which seeing, you no longer perceive, and hearing, you do not understand.

Losing oneself in the knowledge of truth is a very effective escape from realizing one's faults. Church services all over America are packed with psychotics doing that very thing. If they should miss a Sunday or two, the reinforcement breaks down and their guilt starts to catch up with them. But they misinterpret their anxiety, thinking they are guilty for backsliding in attendance.

Psychotics always tend to confuse realizing the truth about their error with *making* an error; that is to say, as soon as they begin to realize their guilt, they believe they are *becoming* guilty for the first time. And if it dawns on them that they are enslaved, they construe it to mean that they are losing their freedom at the very moment of that realization. Psychotics always fancy themselves to be free and good, growing toward perfection, while their entire life is an escape from seeing that the opposite is the case. Proud people resent the truth for showing their way as being the lie that it has always been. It seems to them that their conscience is at fault. They tend to resent the bearer of bad tidings (the innocent, perhaps) as if he had caused them grief. As usual, the remedy for the bad news about themselves is to fall into the psychotic state of disbelief where things seem more to their liking.

Pride comes in through misguided belief. In our psychotic sin-state, our egos must never for one moment believe that we are misguided; so we believe always more deeply *into* the one who lies to us about what we are and all the things we need. For every time we come back to a lover's embrace, every time we make people like us so as to believe in ourselves, we are really losing ourselves in the evil behind the reassurance.

Believing is a form of joining yourself to someone or something. You stubbornly believe what helps make you forget God and feel like God yourself. Belief in evil can save you from good, just as good can save you from evil. There is a complete commitment and involvement either way, depending upon the inclination of the soul.

One of my children developed a way of making me believe in whatever project he had going for him so that he could be released to do and to buy things. Wrong people have no faith in themselves; therefore, they lack motivating power. But they can believe in themselves if you believe in them, and they are freed to have things by that means. This is why psychotics believe in evil—so that evil will believe in them and release them to achieve their secret ambitions.

Believing in a source, whether it is good or evil, opens up your soul to the suggestions of that source. If your soul should change polarity so that you come to love what is right, you can become as naturally good as you are (presently) unnaturally bad.

But now, how can you believe in the truth and be saved by the Divine Presence unless you know how to reach inwardly to where His presence is?

Believe me—like a person, truth is also a sort of environmental presence. The counter-shock of the truth can dissolve the hell identity and transplant into you a new nature. After that initial experience, you will naturally reach within for your reinforcement instead of clinging to people and things. *Such reaching will be inward, silent; the cry of the soul is without voice and without complaint.*

Therefore be warned: complain to anyone and you will draw the comfort of the old sympathy; your roots will grow out into the world and you will continue to become an earthy person.

Once you meditate, all those memories must come to mind which were established through the traumas of worldly reaching and through the comforts you get through such reaching (which can traumatize also). Happily, the power beyond the meditation exercise will wrestle you away, above them, rather than letting you fall into the old patterns of losing yourself in fantasy and pleasure. Just above the refuge of each trauma is the Reality whom you are seeking. The shock of realizing sin purges the sin-memory and establishes the God-memory identity in its stead. After this, you will not reach toward the world for escape and comfort; rather, you will reach within for fulfillment and answers.

Before, you were an enemy of reality. Your ego was on the wrong side, drawing reassurance from other soldiers-of-fortune to frighten off the common enemy of conscience. You drank, sucked in music and smoked pot together, or perhaps you went to church and played bridge together; you supported one another in going the wrong way; you gave each other wrong advice.

Now that you have come over to the other side, you will still be at war. This time you are at variance with the wickedness in the world. Taking your stand, you find life as you draw strength to conquer the enslaving pressure from your embrace of moral principles exuding from the Ever-Presence of inner reality.

Ultimately, salvation depends upon seeing evil as evil and deception as deception, to which you the sinner have joined yourself as the result of believing-into the assumed benefits. The Inner Presence, which shows all things as they are, will expose evil so that you might disbelieve it more perfectly and believe more perfectly in the light, shrinking away from evil's embrace into the bosom of God.

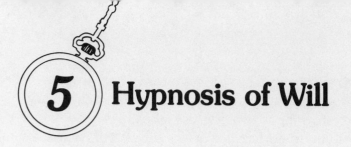

5 Hypnosis of Will

Did you ever try to fix something—anything—and make a booboo? And then, instead of standing back and looking at what a jerk you were, you got mad and tried harder to make it work, only to make a bigger mess. And then what did you do? You repeated the scene over again. Isn't that the story of your life?

Your ego thinks it knows a lot, but upon approaching life, family, business and mechanical problems, you are shocked to discover your ignorance. We start out in life thinking that we are something which we can never really be. We think we have some sort of divine power to will things to happen, and when they backfire and make us look silly, we are threatened. Angrily, we add will to will and frustration to frustration as we keep trying to be that something we are not.

The frustration of resentment happens to be the emotional fuel of willfulness. So when we get mad, our will is energized and projects to the person or thing we are trying to mold or mend.

The part of you that wills things to happen is the flawed, sinning self that never wants to face the truth of its sins, so it loses itself in the symptoms and troubles it creates by reacting against them as if they were the cause. The imperfect thing which evolves mocks your divinity; it challenges you to perfect it and to evolve your perfection in the process.

Your will, inflicted upon others, is a trespass into their minds which causes one of two reactions: rebellion or conformity.

As people conform to your will, you are encouraged to become more willful, and something begins to develop that was not intended. You find you must pay for the glow of pride you get in terms of guilt, frustration and contempt toward people who can't stand up to you. You might even become afraid of your own success, afraid of the conflict that comes from glorying in it, threatened by an easy life without the challenges which your ego needs to grow and know its greatness.

The alternate possibility is that your willfulness may backfire with some people. Those who have a strong will of their own may rebel against you and leave you with egg on your face. Then, pitching your will against theirs again, as well as against obstacles which you yourself have created, becomes a way of life in which you are always growing worse and, at the same time, forgetting what a jerk you are becoming. Frustration is the reward of any effort of will, and that in itself produces a never-ending, self-renewing supply of problems and symptoms that challenges you to perfect your imperfect self.

The energy of a willful, ambitious egomaniac is hostility and frustration—*impatience*, in other words. Impatience is the motivation of a wrong trying to be a right. Impatience is the life of the imperfect person, whereas through patience comes the perfect life from the stillness. Alas, ambition and pride have cut you off from the life of God's love. And so you are left alone, void, without motivation, hunting and pecking for life through responding as an animal to challenges and pressures, conditions which you yourself often cause through the very imperfection of your willing.

The insane ego-claim to perfection lies in dealing with the challenges that result from its own imperfection. Add to this peculiarity of your own nature the cruelties and willfulness of others on the same ego trip, and it is easy to see you will have plenty of aggravation and imperfection in the world to challenge you to roll up your sleeves and prove yourself (while forgetting what a phony you are really becoming).

For every act of will there is a reciprocal frustration-response and trauma. Through trauma (challenges to ego), we evolve a mortal, brutish, individual god-existence apart from God. Yet this ego life of growing and selfishly "coming into our own" is what leads ultimately to our death.

We rarely, if ever, relate the symptoms of failing to ourselves as being the cause. Threatened, we react to their presence, using them to help us grow pridefully in order to forget the sin of pride. The usual technique is to join sides with what we cannot overcome, making enemies into friends and sins into virtues. As the old adage goes, "If you can't lick 'em, join 'em." That is the pattern of our ego life—we give in and glorify what is stronger than us, both with people and with our weaknesses. It is only human nature to take refuge in what we fear. If the enemy cannot be vanquished, we think we can at least keep it from vanquishing us by becoming allies.

Death is the ultimate in a lifetime of concessions, the last payment of a life of sin and pride. As death draws closer and it becomes a problem, we react, struggle against it and perhaps freak out so we don't have to face it. But at long last, we must do what we have always done with enemies stronger than us—give in, like it or not. In order to make it a friend we glorify death, thinking of it as something wonderful we can step across and into, away from shame. Death is exalted and treated the same as every other symptom of pride's failing on the way *to* death.

I started by pointing out that we do not stand back to look at what we are doing objectively. There are only two places where the consciousness can stand in the mind. Most of us have lived in our imagination-mind so long we don't know that another place exists. And we have lived out so many sins from there that we are afraid to come back to the other place, the place of understanding.

Guilt makes us fear the truth. Our need to escape from guilt drives us to seek comfort in that through which guilt came (sin). Therefore, the compelling power of any form of temptation is our *own unwillingness* to face what we have become. The more guilty we become, the more attractive pleasure is. We become more and more fascinated with evil itself in order to get it to hold our attention away and so to relieve guilt feelings. We can't and won't stand back because we are afraid to be free from the comfort of our sins.

Were you to allow yourself to come back to this other place inside, you might realize what is wrong with the way you exist. And were your soul grieved to repentance, you would come alive in a new way through realizing more and more. Truth (conscience) would then become your friend and guide, and not your enemy, as it is in the sin/death-as-life existence.

Life comes through from the place of understanding. Understanding, which comes from the soul's seeking to know God intimately, firsthand, has a different quality than mere secondhand information from books.

I refer here to spiritual understanding, life which comes from within. But our present existence has arisen because of the fall away from our spiritual environment, for which we are compensating in flesh and in carnal knowledge from the natural world.

The connecting link to sin is pride, and the life of pride is based on emotional excitement. When you do not will God's divine will and purpose and respond to it, you have instead a will to power (ambition). And because things which build your ego become too important to you, you begin growing and dreaming through responding to temptation objects. That, briefly, is how your ego becomes cut off from reality and comes to realize a selfish, separate, prideful existence centered around greed and desire.

Men of understanding have no need to find the life which comes from seeking excitement, because they are content with the life which comes from abiding in God's love. The need for excitement (love and hate) represents the ego's need to grow apart from God in order to realize itself as God. We escape from the life of understanding (doing the will of God and being molded in His likeness) to a willful but morbid existence of our own. And such a life, sustained by the corrupting source of excitement, is sin. Furthermore, that intelligence which rises to cater inventively to our need to be God, is evil. Response to evil is necessary for this kind of life; otherwise there is no base, no contact, no energy to separate us from God the Reality and to evolve an individual soul-body with its separate, independent, prideful existence.

If animals had understanding, they could never grow and develop the way they do now. Wisdom would be their protection from stress and danger, and hence from the need to compensate.

So it is an exciting thing *not to understand,* because then we blunder. Reacting to the stressful effect of our own folly and blindness, we respond and grow as animals do. And all this responding and growing appears to be an adventure toward some imagined advantage or greatness.

Before you read on, please take note of the basic theme of this text: response, wherein you find life, is obedience; and it is *always* obedience, whether you are responding to good or to evil. Response takes away one life and replaces it with an existence centered in the other. And most important, which one we respond to has something to do with what we believe when our ego is appealed to. Such is the nature of salvation *from* sin and salvation *for* sin.

Before you can find God's salvation, you must fully understand your own ego-weakness as it relates to each particular sin-symptom. You must come to realize exactly what is wrong with your attitude and the way you are going and growing, and you must resolve those responses at each point along the way.

To realize, you must desire to realize. Your motivation must be the reverse of what caused your fall. You must be ready to do the divine will rather than will your own independent existence apart from God as God yourself. And within the realization itself is the power to change— you need struggle no more. It will happen in its own time.

As I said before, the sinful life requires the service of that (intelligence) which understands and caters to your need to become God. Without evil and its special kind of knowledge, a separate sin-existence is no more possible than the moon separating from earth's gravity without the presence of another heavenly body.

In order to experience our own life of pride, we must completely abandon the understanding which inhibits the soul, and never stand back lest we experience conflict, pain and shame. Pride cannot coexist with the pride-resolving, problem-resolving presence of understanding. Pride can only survive in the distracting, exciting presence of evil and error, to which we owe our first allegiance and to which we are fixated and addicted. Void of understanding, which gives true life and growth, we crave knowledge, which gives false life and growth. And rote knowledge, whether about good or evil, whether true or false, is always used in a very special way to swell the ego and excite the body to grow.

Because you have exciting, self-glorifying goals, you start responding to what is wrong—to that which promises to make your willful dreams come true. From that point on, you are manipulated through your growing needs and wants.

Because we have rejected or not found the life and breath of the Spirit, our willfulness compels us to escape and reinforce the sinful life through traumas based on temptation and false knowledge. For no soul has a life unless it shares the life of its source; it has no other knowledge except to share the knowledge of its source, no other permanence except to share the permanence of its source, and no other identity except the identity to which it responds and mirrors.

The stubborn, prideful soul, "awakening" on the lower plane through excitement, prefers to escape shame, journeying towards its own reality through more excitement. Thus begins the adventure of evolving ego-selfhood. Because we will not stand in the other place to see otherwise, there always seems to be hope in that which leads to death.

The challenges we create by the problems we cause set afire the wheel of nature, the cycle of life and death. Slowly but surely, we begin evolving an ego-selfhood in an earth-bonded soul-body. And even beyond dying, we keep seeking the illusive eternal living that is part of the promise of becoming a god.

The *payment for sin is death,* but Satan has a way of making death seem to be the entrance to heaven. And we are compelled to believe that, or face up to the truth about pride and death.

The mind of the sinning soul acts like an environment to him. The sinner reacts and grows, and through every reaction and intrigue of his own mind he continues to forget what grew and still grows. Because it is unnatural for a person to grow and evolve like a beast, there is conflict. And because it is even more unnatural to live from and to hide in the imagination, there is more conflict.

Remember that trauma is what every sinner needs in order to grow. However, the memories of traumas (which stick in our craw and remind us of our failing and sin) can also be used for escape. Because they threaten

92

the soul with guilt and shame, memories can excite (through resentment) in exactly the same way as did the real-life traumas which caused the memories to stick. A traumatic memory is a little piece of the identity of an environment or person that got inside us, so the outside environment became an inside environment—hence the conflict and threat to our egos.

If you have ever been bothered by recurring memories flickering in the light of conscience, you have surely noticed how it upsets you again and again to think of those who upset you before. One more upset (judgment) can help you forget the guilt of the last upset because the mind is a world in which you can relive and reuse memories of experiences just as if they were happening again in reality. Thus, escape artists can use their environment to supply their imagination-environment and later recreate the trauma/escape/growth experience in a way more to their liking. We pride ourselves in emotions which let sin enter, and then we emotionally pride ourselves in reviving and reliving the past.

I have already pointed out that resentment which rises in response to environment is like an emotional candy bar. For a short season, it can recharge and renew the false life (based upon emotions), even as it can appear to make you innocent. But there is a point where you become afraid of the very experience you need, and you start feeding on your own juices as you resent and relive the scenes in your head. So you think about the things which excite, upset and otherwise turn on your animal self in order to escape into the comforting folds of emerging feeling and sensuality.

Naturally, the favorite trauma-producing memory of

man is woman. He thinks about her continually as a means of excitement to escape from what grew up in him from the last woman-based experience. And he can renew his ego life in her image-presence to escape being enslaved to her personal presence. All who sin are slaves, you see! But there is no real escape in imagery, for the evil lurking in the image exists now in his own mind, egging him on in fantasy to power and glory.

And now sir, as you disintegrate—angry, bitter and fearful of new adventures with women as well as other excitements and traumas, and with nothing to look forward to—you go back into your mind, away from reality, fondling the memories of all your traumas, reviving emotions in order to escape the reality of the "hound of heaven" (conscience). However, because there is no real experience in your imagination world to reinforce your rotten ego-self, *your mind feeds on itself* as it absorbs you into past scenes, and you waste away to nothing, often through cancer.

Resist not evil (don't respond). Grow, now, by overcoming (coming over) stress—by *not responding*, in other words. Through love of understanding, become immune to stress instead of absorbing it. Find the true life through realizing away the ego-sin of emotion. Learn how to go through experiences without letting experiences go through you. Through patience, seal out the evil world, the trauma-based order of growing and being.

Calmness is a threat to the ego because the ego thrives on emotion through motion. Be still, and discover the spiritual life as you give up the ego-emotional life.

Every time you are patient, your conscious mind becomes a little more free from the terrible grip of trauma.

Now your appreciation of the highly intelligent order behind your patient response grows. Greater appreciation becomes faith in what is true. Knowing (understanding) and believing the truth sets you free.

Faith is the response to what one deeply knows is right (the spiritual order within) that cancels out the obedience to the world. You learn by unlearning. Your strength and character grow in direct proportion to your patience (non-response to the world).

Every day that you live perceiving these delicate principles, which cannot be learned or taught, will edge you closer to the timeless moment where there is no response whatsoever. When that time arrives you will be the matter of life, and death will be no more. Indeed, the very last enemy to be conquered is death. To get there, you must abandon the traumatic, emotional, illusory way of life which leads down to death. You must give up, as a living sacrifice, the brutish ego-life and breath which is based on being emotionally involved with temptation.

Permit me to repeat this theme again, and forgive me for being redundant. I really do not wish to press these words upon you by sheer repetition. I know, above all, that mere academic learning can never save you. In my repetition is the hope that you will one day understand. I write to leave a trail of clues designed to awaken you, to help you to comprehend more fully the error while you are on your way to the light.

Let us together reexamine the point I made about the life of pride being built on emotional *response* to temptation. Falling, the dying ego comes alive in sin as it dies to truth. Emotion rises as the soul falls, and this trauma triggers and sustains the evolution of the ego/animal mortal life. Animal emotion (such as anger) then becomes the driving force of the fallen ego. The psychological term for this supportive, primitive animal energy is "libido." Response to the world, due to the appeal to your ego, liberates the soul from its spiritual response-ability, growth and life. After that, you are compulsive about emotion.

Emotion is the breath of life to the evolving fallen nature. Pressure from any form of temptation takes over and reinforces the growth of the mortal, prideful self. Emotion happens to be the ego's way of forgetting the ugly (dying) thing that grew out of the last emotional experience, so you grow to *need* your emotional-pressure source.

Emotion is the evidence of pride sinning and reviving itself, and emotion again triggers a morbid growth factor. And because that emotional response also produces an element of forgetfulness of conscience, you can use trauma to think yourself innocent. Once lost in the emotional thought process, you cannot see much wrong with yourself.

For this reason, guilty people take pleasure in any form of pressure: being backed against the wall, being mad, cheated or upset—any form of excitement will do. The hope of the ego lies in all those experiences which in reality lead to death. Because the psychotic will not and therefore cannot see the truth, and because evil reinforces both the sin life and the forgetfulness of it, what actually kills him appears to be saving him.

There is this built-in morbidness which makes itself felt at the end of every emotional cycle, but the sinner counteracts the realization by dreaming ahead about new adventures, excitements or troubles. Fearing the truth in the stillness, never for one moment will the living-it-up (down, really) soul allow itself to rest. The restless soul demands the next excitement of love or hate, often even before the old one has grown cold.

The psychotic's emotional fascination with evil is due to his pride in individualism, which is the emotional/animal ego-life apart from God. The excitement that meets the egotist's need to grow away from God to be God himself, makes it appear to him that he is somehow in charge of his destiny. Rising and catering to the occasion of this need, temptation excites him to experience forgetfulness of the true life as it reinforces the false life.

The Good Book has many references to the enslaving love and life that the world offers. We are admonished to be in the world but not of it. And in another place it says, "Be not conformed to the world, but be transformed through the renewing of your mind from within." And again it says that whosoever shall preserve his life (the animal life and breath) shall lose his life (the spiritual life and breath). "But whosoever shall lose his life for My sake (give up his animal life and breath), shall find life." Those are the words of the Messiah. Indeed, were His words deeply *understood,* they would lead to true eternal life as the extension of this life.

Rejecting the life of the light, the soul responds and takes its nature from sin, whereupon a death-oriented soul-body appears, grows old, becomes diseased and dies.

But real life beckons in the opposite direction. It comes through the remolding of the mind from within, through not conforming to pressures, ego appeals and the entice-ments of the world, but inclining toward what is wise, true, fair and just, being very careful not to become proud, even in this.

Therefore must you abide, neither responding nor

causing response in others. Measure your enslavement to sin and death by the degree to which you respond and cause response, because to that degree are you a slave and do you enslave others.

Emotion is the "sweetness" of the ego/animal life. Suffer, therefore, the pain of denying yourself this candy and receive instead the life of the Spirit.

As I said before, psychotics (sinners) "control" their growth by interacting emotionally with people and things. The lifestyle which ends in death depends upon the sweet trauma of drama. I called trauma response, and response I called obedience. Closeness to death can be measured by that very sensitivity to what mortal man cherishes as "life."

Mastery of life is in direct proportion to the natural control you have over your emotions. A diminishing response represents a diminishing ego-need for emotional vitality. Such control is not a control in the ordinary sense, whereby you exert some kind of effort or discipline. It comes from your soul's willingness to give up the emotional breath of life that your ego needs to preserve the individuality of your pride separate from God as a god yourself. *You must give up your willfulness in exchange for willingness.*

The natural control I refer to comes from the life which comes through stillness, as opposed to the life which comes from activity, and through doing what we know is right from within.

Hold fast therefore to noble principles. Cease taking your character and substance from the evil behind every excitement and pressure. Temptation is excitement; excitement is trauma, and trauma is the evolution of ego-becoming. All of this is sin, the way of life that leads to death.

Conversely, the delicate realization of every simple and noble principle leads to seeing it through. Living through experiences without taking energy from them frees the soul from its enslavement to sin and death. The soul is raised to flash progressively upon greater and more subtle principles and the creative force operating behind them. That in turn breaks down the fleshly, sensual, emotional bond with death and hell, and leads to great inner strength, patience and love, which, expressed another way, is a dying to death and to the appeal of temptation.

To give up your emotional excitement of love and hate is to give up the substance of ego/animal life and breath (which is nothing more than the life that leads to death). To give up the life-breath experience upon which the ego is built is to die to the foundation of sin. And it will indeed appear that you are giving up not only natural life, but eternal life also. Happy is he who can give up this "life" with no guarantee of another, because this marvelous thing can only be done strengthened by God's love.

As the Scripture says, unless a man die and be born again, he cannot enter the Kingdom of God. Such a "death" is preferred by all seekers. They alone are graced to die to death and to the false immortality of their mortality.

The hard-core hell/death/woman-centered psychotic/ egomaniac can never abandon his lie-based ego life, for it is all he has and all he cares to know. The beast man cannot bear to become nothing in order to become something of God. He can only become the deluded something that is destined to dissolve to a nothing. He is fascinated with evil excitements, forever lost in the traumas of his prideful way of becoming and forgetting the sin of it. The last forgetting, through the last comfort, is the trauma of death. And the drawing spirit of the life that leads to hell beyond death is Satan.

The power trauma has to reinforce identity and to relieve one of guilt makes it a comfort. Trauma is the heartbeat of many things: ego-life, comfort, self-righteousness, false innocence, growth and pride; but, on the other side of the ledger, it eventually manifests in guilt, depression, fear, anxiety and suffering—death.

Again, I must tell you that I am writing to you to leave a trail of clues and I implore you not to study me. Scan these words. Scan the Scriptures for understanding. BUT NEVER STUDY OR BE ABSORBED IN MERE WORDS. Search for clues. Become awakened and more fully appreciate the way. See clearly the appeal to your ego and the subtlety of your next emotional response.

On the way back to reality, you will be patient and non-judgmental a thousand, thousand times, and every time you will appreciate more deeply the principle of patience. You will more fully grasp the significance of the power and majesty behind heaven unrolling before you on earth. You will see hell barred and bridled more surely.

After the initial pains of self-denial have passed, you will grow from the inner light. Here you will find no boredom or futility; you will not fear the guilt that seems to come from doing nothing. Doing nothing is where you discover life, new somethings to grow toward.

As you sit quietly, you may feel guilt which seems to come from wasting time, and you will want to rush away from it into activity. Instead, know that Reality is present, revealing your nature to you. Guilt makes you want to escape into your mind, or rush away to seek excitement in order to forget sin; but if you will bear the pain of being still and let the moment pass, you will find the true innocence and true life that come through awareness.

6 Murder by Knowledge

There are rapists who are psychopathic enough to feel that their victims benefit from being violated.

But sexual rape is not the only kind there is; one can rape the soul, mind and body with religion, education and with drugs. And rape is not only rape when it is forced and violent. Seduction is also rape, whereby through deception you find in yourself what is not supposed to be there.

There are classes of social psychopaths who, like the sex rapist, feel that they are doing you a service when they violate you with education, religion, politics and medicine.

The "benefit" of rape, whether by seduction or by sudden violent pressure, is the special creation of a new identity and reality for the victim. For, once violated, the victim tends to cling to vile rapists of all kinds for reassurance through escape and for identity reinforcement (in the same moment of escape). Psychopaths pride themselves in being creators of sick realities for sick personalities (all the while pretending to enrich your life).

Afraid of truth, all psychotic victims are indeed fascinated with the reassurances of evil. Being drawn hypnotically toward the familiar spirit makes them its legal prey; a bad conscience makes every temptation attractive. Victims are drawn like moths to a candle because the violently-implanted identity craves the comfort of the rapist "parent" that gave it life. Seeking refuge from one psychopath, you become involved with others. Unless you find something called understanding, there is no salvation, no escape from wicked-shepherd, letter-of-the-law authorities.

The syndrome is something like having a fight with a woman and making up in bed. Any violation through violence, pressure or tease has a way of making itself familiar. Being raped is like undergoing psychic judo— you trip, you fall, you cling to what tripped you because that's all there is left to give you support, and you fall harder.

Would you believe it—if you were violated by fire, you would find ordeal-by-fire attractive and you would seek fulfillment by fire. Psychopaths know this principle well.

Do you know what welders often do when they get burned? They put the torch close to the burn for comfort. They call that pulling the heat out of the burn. Would you do that sort of thing if you were burned? Some people would, and the reason why has something to do with the way they react, with whether or not they were violated by the experience.

Now this principle applies to everything in life, especially education. Are you going to learn in such a way that you lose yourself in what you are doing so much that it becomes you and cries out for the rapist?

Some rapists are psychopaths, others are psychotic

puppets carrying out orders, compulsively acting out a dream and dramatizing the character of their models. They kill because the captain ordered the sergeant to order the soldier, and the soldier cannot refuse. Amazing how one man—the general—can move an entire army to its death, and the whole army cannot oppose the general.

When we are violated, that which disturbed us becomes the basis, the foundation, of what we are and what we are going to be. And no matter how vile that potential is, it is all we have. To lose the assurances of our corrupter/model seems like ceasing to exist. The baring of the guilt-stained soul to the light is more torture than we can bear. If sinning and killing pleases our master, then we kill for the relief of his embrace.

Like Communists who brainwash people by making them study Mao Tse-tung's book, so do false religions and false education create a robot-elite by forced study. From six to eighteen years of age, children are required to sit six hours a day listening to some impatient bore instead of being outside, learning and playing through experience and curiosity. No wonder our children are mad, bad and sick.

Since time immemorial it has been said that knowledge opens new worlds. We are persuaded or forced (for our own "good") to learn everything we can because knowledge is supposed to liberate the mind. That concept is certainly very appealing, for it is almost perfectly true— but not quite because, in fact, only the *truth* can set you free. Pridefully acquired *knowledge* merely liberates the soul from understanding.

But surely truth and factual knowledge are the same, aren't they? The answer is that although they should

105

complement one another, they can, through seduction and pressure, become separated and lead in opposite directions. People can learn themselves *away* from understanding. Haven't you heard the old saying, "all knowledge and no common sense"? Knowledge minus understanding is prideful, hypnotic and traumatic. However, knowledge *can* lead to awakening and to understanding, and when it does, knowledge ceases.

When knowledge leads you up to understanding and is no more, understanding takes over, replacing the dependency upon knowledge with the wholesome dependency upon self-understanding. Since it involves growing through discovery, understanding sets you free from knowledge and from the need to memorize; it delivers you from dusty old teachers and books. It is precisely for this reason that understanding threatens authorities; this is why they selfishly force you to learn.

If everyone had understanding, who would need authorities? Who would need problem solvers if we could solve our own problems? Psychopaths perpetuate their leadership by leading you *away* from understanding.

When knowledge can be held out to appear greater than understanding, then he who tempts through knowledge leads with knowledge. And so, as victims in bondage through knowledge, we are set apart from the understanding of how we have been tricked and what has gone wrong with our lives.

And by way of the tree of knowledge here we are, lost in the learning trap, bewildered and confused. And now all that rises to solve the problems caused by being lost in knowledge is more knowledge, and more bondage to the serpent of knowledge. And so we sink in a mire of despair.

Are you beginning to understand the appeal of knowledge to your ego and its power over you?

If you are forced or coerced to study or concentrate too hard, too long, on anything, good or bad, your attention becomes so involved, so lost, so hypnotized, that it can't get back to where it was. Because of the terrible errors of judgment made under that spell, you may be unable, even afraid to come back to the reality from whence you fell. A variation of this same principle lies behind every pleasure of sin. False security and relief from guilt come from being more completely involved with whatever or whoever holds your attention ever more perfectly. And this is especially true with study; you can temporarily relieve the inferiority from the guilt of study by studying ever harder.

Whether you realize it or not, concentration is not a way of improving yourself; it is a way of giving up your soul to attain some imagined ego-objective. Fascination is the second stage of concentration. Here your ego becomes relieved of the guilt of achieving through being more and more completely captivated by ideas and concepts. To capture anyone's soul, then, you must get him to try, will and want, and then you can trap him through his imagination. (Another form of this is to encourage egos to imagine "creatively," later to fantasize and to escape.) Now if you try hard to do something, the same thing happens. When you realize the truth about trying, you might try not to try, but that is still trying. Trying to solve your problem by trying causes more anxiety about the problem because will is still involved.

The razor's-edge difference between knowledge and deep understanding is the difference between doing it the

107

easy or the hard way, and between life and death.

To seek to know oneself as God amid the knowledge of one's own mind happens to be the original sin. Permit me now to lay bare the subtle terror which lurks behind book-learning as opposed to understanding for yourself.

There is a killer system in this world, the sole purpose of which is to trick you into being proud in order to capture you through knowledge and defeat your unfoldment through understanding. The serpent of the knowledge tree is still around, enticing us toward glory through knowledge, mocking our innocence. The parasitical human agencies who subscribe willfully to that system are programmed to destroy your understanding for the sake of their power over you. They will try their damnedest to displace the spirit of the word (understanding), which leads toward life, with the letter of the word (the spirit behind knowledge), which leads to death. Having been converted, you too will begin to reflect, cling to and serve the serpent spirit of the dry-knowledge system.

Without realizing the danger, and thinking it to be advantageous, vast numbers of people revel in corruption by opening wide their mouths and allowing religion to be shoved down their throats. The reason is that, once separated from an intuitive source of knowing and being, the vain and the fallen crave knowledge to distract and to fill the void of their souls; it is their way of forgetting to realize. The spirit that rises to "save" you with knowledge is always that which felled with knowledge.

Knowledge, then, begins to substitute for understanding and facts become imaginary name-things into which you can escape from understanding. You forget (guilt) in one way by remembering in another. To involve your willful self in thinking and in worry provides relief from truth as well as renewed hope for the forbidden things of glory and power.

To *think* hard about anything provides an almost perfect escape from realizing its deeper meaning. It is easy to fool ourselves into believing that we are seeking truth when we look to knowledge for truth, because just as the appeal of knowledge can lead astray, so can more of it lead you from realizing the sin of it. And that is just as true of knowledge about good things as it is of the knowledge of evil.

With the fall to knowledge comes the guilt of pride, and the guilty nature, retreating from understanding which exposes guilt, finds refuge in more knowledge, excuses, rationale, verses and chapters, and educational escapism.

In all psychotic positive-thinking/learning episodes, knowledge similar to understanding rises in the mind in such a way that it seems to originate from within. Knowledge enveloping your soul in this way makes your ego feel as if it were the divine source of truth. The kind of knowledge that lends itself to getting lost in makes you "high." But no matter whether it is emotionally or intellectually induced, any high becomes the next low, attended by more guilt.

With knowledge comes guilt; through understanding comes innocence.

Guilt and inferiority are caused by the conflict between what we have become through knowledge and what we might have become through understanding. Alas, through ambition or weakness we have become prisoners of the spirit behind knowledge and we can't (or won't) get back.

Knowledge, which causes sin, then appears in different

guises as if to save us from sin. Without the benefit of understanding, our feelings of emptiness and inadequacy get twisted around and interpreted to mean that our solution lies in more knowledge. You can be intimidated into thinking that you don't know enough, and tricked into wanting to be with people who are supposed to know. We look to accomplished, lettered men of science and religion to save us. And that is the knowledge trap.

Even when you are "into" sound philosophic truths, you are rarely threatened by what such lofty words *mean.* The excitement of learning tends to draw the ego deeper into a psychotic sleep that prevents the awakening to meaning; instead, we awaken in a dream universe amid comforting, lofty word-things. So it comes to pass that we can *know* truth egotistically, without really realizing or being intimate with truth at all. All we have are noises and image-things in our heads which are real to us, memories that one day fall apart at the grave, laying bare the evil spirit of knowledge behind them.

Pure understanding threatens the worldly-wise. All psychotic egos, ambitiously aspiring to the godhead, avoid (through *trauma-learning*) the allegiances and moral responsibilities that go with understanding. Prideful learning (similar to worry) blocks understanding, giving us the freedom to pretend to be good when we are not. When it suits us, we can be conditioned to gloss over a multitude of sins with such rigid, conditioned, *learned* moral values.

Before I go on, allow me to run through the principle of evolutionary compensation through knowledge once more.

Any excitement or pressure creates a psychotic, emotional state of involvement with the intelligence behind that pressure which frees the prideful soul from reality to evolve physically and spiritually separate from God, with an earthy, independent ego-life and mortal selfhood. Through the challenges and problems caused by self-seeking through knowledge, a false, selfish type of concern and cunning evolves which passes for goodness and intelligence. As in all psychotic episodes, the soul eludes its guilt amid evolving knowledge-answers. We don't want simple answers; we need complexity to maintain our pride.

The illusion of progress is almost perfect, except that every upset or shock which evolves an answer also produces greater problems. Eventually, when our own systems fail miserably, we substitute other people's knowledge-answers. But what really is the basic nature of any ego-answer? It is always a more complete involvement with mind (through emotion), aiming for grandeur (at best), but settling for "innocence" (at least). If we can't be great ourselves, we can at least be grateful to those who help ease our guilt.

In any kind of growing, one solves one problem only to discover another. But the egotist, developing in vanity, discovers problems of his own making that challenge him to compensate by producing the kind of complex knowledge-answers that never should have existed. This leads to an ultimate enslavement to science and technology, behind which sits the god of knowledge, laughing up his sleeve at the dehumanization of man.

The lives of students everywhere are imperiled by the kind of pressured growing and learning aimed at creating a feudal system of zombies who are forbidden to see for themselves and who must look to Big Brother for everything. "Good students" are nearly all potential traitors to humanity. As temporary or permanent enemies of understanding, they are destined to become the next generation of hierarchical, ecclesiastical, letter-of-the-law parents and teachers without any patience for those seeking to understand.

When I was a child, I was slow to grasp. Because my understanding forbade me to learn in the way of the world, I can still understand life today. Because I wanted to get to the bottom of what was taught me, I was very slow to learn; but I got through and I am speaking to you now from the other side, and the other side is testifying to where I am coming from.

All the children of ambition are blind, unprincipled, beastly, mercilessly cruel achievers. If they are not our social keepers and bureaucratic puppets, they are psychopathic or psychotic killers, taking pride in tearing down what made them (or destroyed them). Any kind of learning without the benefit of understanding builds pride. The evil pride-thing operating through knowledge hardens the heart; it dehumanizes as it teaches. (Even street knowledge makes the rebel proud.)

Sensitive drop-outs (by and large more intelligent than the cop-outs) often become anti-social. Some cannot learn because of a total revolution against the rape of pressure-teaching. Their minds erect emotional barriers to protect against being made over in the image of the mad spirit of education. Alas, they have the mad spirit nevertheless. To respond, even in rebellion, is to obey; we are what we hate or love (cling to).

Although knowledge does seem to be the enemy, the real enemy is always the pressure-spirit *behind* knowledge; our weakness—the struggle for it or the struggle against it—lets it in.

The system that projects its vileness into a child in the first place, looks at him as though *he* were the problem in the second place. The pathetic plight of every victim challenges and justifies the system to give more foul, soul-killing "help." Therefore, the vile spirit of the rote-learning system hardens the soul in its revolt against being "helped" by the parent/teacher/minister, but rebellion only gives power to false authorities, making it seem as if they have the right to shove religion, educational brainwashing and criminal reform down the victims' throats. Conversely, rebels who have become decadent and vile through their rebellion, enjoy their contempt for hypocrisy in order to maintain their "innocence" and their right to destroy through rebellion. The more the wicked system tries to help, the bigger the sickness it creates, which then seems to need its help—you know, "after all, the kids can't read," type of thing. The cure is the sickness. The "help" of the world is a hindrance to meaningful change, and the victims of such assistance generally go mad either trying to make it or rebelling. Through taxes, research and special programs, we are being made to finance our own destruction.

Even though right things are sometimes taught (the right numbers, verses and chapters reeled off and behavior patterns drilled in) *the spirit of the system projects its own secret vileness at the very moment it pretends to reform.* Hell's projection through the neurotic application of knowledge is ignorance, crime, revolution, disease, famine, war, and all manner of tragedy.

The trademark of evil is pressure. It violates and

creates the need for more of the same. Pressure is calculated to drive out understanding and make one dependent on it as the ground of one's knowing and being.

Decisions made under emotional duress and pressure, whether in rebellion or conformity to it, always favor the pressure sources. Having fallen prey to the excitement of temptation, we find ourselves subject to the excitement of pressure. We come to need pressure to function, to make decisions, to learn, to escape and to maintain rebellion.

Just as conformity to the system mysteriously destroys the soul, even so does rebellion. As victims, we do not realize that while knowledge may be blocked through resentment-based rebellion, the identity behind the pressure gets inside us nevertheless. The struggle for or the struggle against amounts to the pathos of your ego willing and trying, concentrating, fixated in such a way that you are drawn deeper into the hypnosis of your sin.

Criminals become on the outside what hypocrites are like on the inside. And now, between the two extremes giving power to one another, they evolve hell's miserable world into existence, blocking out the plan of heaven on earth which could come through the space of patient understanding.

The hell you see around you evolved through hypocrisy, through the misuses of law, religion and science. And it is your willful struggling to save yourself egotistically that compels you to work against your own best interest.

Even though you personally might desire a life of understanding, those who are threatened by it can block you from the light if you resent them, trapping you to trust and rely on them through that resentment. The inferiority that attends the emotion of resentment (because of having become upset and judgmental) can unconsciously drive you to compensate by living up to what they want for you, or to best them with some kind of achievement requiring evolution and knowledge. Since any compensation always causes more guilt than it cures, you can even come to fear being better. So it comes to pass that knowledge can cause ignorance.

Resentment toward your mother can set you up to want what she wants for you, to please her and placate her pressure. And later, the pain of achievement can cause you to fear what it does to you and thus to reject that achievement and become a failure in order to "get even" with mother; but that itself is another form of trying, dreaming and achieving, even if what you become is an alcoholic (or worse).

The spirit of reform is the selfsame spirit that has created most insanity and criminality. *Such a system does not ever intend to reform or cure anyone.* Through its serpent-like hypocrisy and artificial, contrived rules, regulations and answers, it slyly hardens, cripples and finally kills you. The answer is simple—just observe, watch, trust what you realize about others and yourself. Don't rebel or conform. No need to do anything—wait.

Social psychopaths rising as reformers and teachers are ever seeking more and more power to strangle the life, selfhood and freedom of the masses. The power-hungry elite are determined to make mankind dependent upon them for answers. Our growing needs cry out for them to dig down into their dark, bottomless intellects to the hell which lives in them and on our dying to them.

Is it so hard to believe that there exists a class of beings to whom, in our sin, we are delivered to suffer unto death or to awakening?

It has been said that the devil is an ape, and that he is also a gentleman. Social psychopaths can rise to power quickly because their unprincipled natures allow them to rapidly memorize and mimic. Such smiling Hitlers are threatened by the brightness of an understanding child. They all know that their time is short, for enlightenment is coming to this dark world. And when it does, understanding will overcome the tin gods of knowledge-power who live off our dying to them for answers.

No need to try, no need to struggle. Just watch everyone challenging, teasing and tempting you; put a distance between you and them. Look—don't learn. Just scan, appreciate, watch. You will come to realize what you need to know—that's all. Wait until that realizing works its way through you EFFORTLESSLY.

Do you see why the rapist-forces can impatiently "teach" one kind while destroying another? Those who are destroyed are often the most suited to project on earth a peaceful, heavenly kingdom. The vile system is never threatened by all us confused, confounded victims; it is flattered by the conformist and strengthened by the rebel—that is, 'til comes the day of the rebel, the time when the hell created by the matrix of hypocrisy breaks loose, as it surely will. For the seeds of destruction are within every prideful building.

I cannot bring my message to the rulers of the world. I cannot go to the behavioral scientists and say, "Look what you are doing to all the little children with your meaningless, boring teaching methods and pressures." *They will not and cannot see what they are doing wrong.* (But our end is just, for we elect the kind of leaders we deserve.)

Psychopaths exist to trap, confuse, confound, dehumanize and destroy mankind by hook or by crook. That is what they are created to do. The psychopathic spirit of technology is calculated to make us fall again and again to need more knowledge. Remember, all solutions without understanding cause never-ending challenges that raise hell with its knowledge to the rescue. But knowledge cannot save, because it is a bog and not clear water. And the life of the troll in the bog depends upon your budding ego falling into the knowledge swamp.

Knowledge causes problems, problems cause challenges and challenges cause the animal evolution of ego-selfhood.

The social bureaucracy and the Mafia are both examples of successful self-perpetuating systems of psychopaths and psychotics working together as a team. All such organizations are hell-based, even though some of them may wear the respectable cloak of legality. Education, for example, has evolved to where it can be seen as the absurd, heartless thing it was all along, requiring us to learn the useless, or the useful *made* useless and boring.

Not only do wicked authorities feel justified in impatiently pushing knowledge down "lazy" students' throats, forcing them to learn garbage that cannot possibly be of any practical value in life, but when students try to grasp what is understandable, the teacher is also impatient. Such a teacher has the terrible power to make a sincere desire to understand seem all wrong. That attitude can upset a student, making him doubt his own sanity and become afraid of inquiry. Without an alternative to learning in the teacher's way, he cannot learn at all.

Two million juveniles were arrested in 1976, and that is

only those who were *caught.*

This is the age of the psychopaths. They have evolved the authority to change your children into rebels, murderers, thieves and dope addicts or social climbers—self-righteous, characterless zombies and weaklings whose lives revolve around the lie of knowledge. The most intelligent children, those most fitted to rule and guide, those who might one day govern and teach intelligently, *are being systematically destroyed* through pressure. A death-centered, upside-down system is evolving where the slimy thing in the bottomless pit is emerging on top as a god, with terrible power through knowledge.

The scum of the earth rule and control, *and their greatest enemy is the enlightenment and perception of understanding souls.* We are made out to be mad. *We* are treated for the "sickness" of sanity. *We* are different. In America alone, ten thousand children are slaughtered every year by impatient parents.

Laid bare before your eyes are two diametrically opposed systems which are, to all intents and purposes, apparently alike in their knowledge of science, religion, politics, human rights and law, except that one of them is diabolically evil. The evil psychopath often hides behind knowledge and respectability, and wherever he can, he will subtly betray, destroy, confound and mock those with understanding. The devil is who you elect and love, for he is the model of everything you want to be.

Academe is the mortal enemy of individual, independent, intuitive learning through discovery. So much so that when two different scientists possessing the same knowledge and training oppose one another on vital issues, the psychopath will always maintain that what is dangerous is safe, and what is safe is dangerous. The atomic power controversy is the perfect example of this kind of thing.

The social psychopath is a subtle killer, one way or another. If he succeeds in becoming a justice of the Supreme Court, he will give clemency to the undeserving and be merciless to those who he perceives are innocent. He commits injustice with justice, protected behind the book he goes by.

And so, while knowledge could be presented in the simplest way, it is purposely complicated so that the mind cannot grasp the reality behind it. The rote system gives no choice. It forces you to learn *and accept the spirit of learning* or reject knowledge altogether. Continued pressure keeps you from understanding how to cope. Does this not explain the plight of the so-called autistic children who are withdrawing into themselves?

See then the two ways, and see one in the light of the other. Behold the counterfeit which presents truth and justice in such a way that the mind becomes blocked to realizing and acting in its own best interest. Whether you react with conformity or rebellion, a prideful nature comes into existence—a slave revolving, evolving and devolving around the hell which tempted it into creation.

The hell-system applies steady pressure from the day of your birth to your death to keep you in a psychotic sleep, to know only what it teaches you. You may resist its suggestions, but never its spirit. Rebellion, you see, is merely the other way to conform, wherein you become suggestible to the criminal psychopath who comforts you like family in your contrary lifestyle.

Without understanding to modify what we hear, we

are all suggestible as hell.

As a seeker, you are in conflict because, although you may hear the truthful facts, you sense danger. You see that knowledge is dry and dead, and that rote learning takes something away; but your resentment, blocking enlightenment and knowledge, makes you feel inferior for not being like others. All around, people are gobbling it all up, getting ahead and apparently prospering. Your sensibility is assaulted and overwhelmed; you become confused and confounded, doubting your own ability and sanity.

Now hear this: *being made to doubt what is right in the heart is shades of original sin!* Knowledge has pressure-power to force us (through an inherited emotional hold on the mind) to doubt what is true and trap us into wanting and reaching for more knowledge. Psychopaths have this inherited power of suggestion to persuade and confound, to make us more lost than we are already. Now it is one thing to revel in pressure because your ego enjoys that kind of service, but it is another thing to be emotionally and unwillingly *trapped* into the pride-of-ambition game.

The serpent spirit of culture is responsible for millions of drop-outs and misfits who have tried to reject the pressure-system of learning and religion as a way of preserving their selfhood. How were they to know that rebellion is another trap, taking you out of the frying pan into the fire. How were they to know that you can't escape through rebellion? Whether you like the system or hate it, you evolve through it to serve the hell of it, taking pride in all sorts of "good knowledge," and also excusing yourself with the bad knowledge gained from more honestly wicked company.

120

The warning of the prophet comes echoing down to us through the corridors of time—"The letter killeth, but the Spirit giveth life."

For God's sake, parents, don't let your children fall into the vile hands of the letter-people:

the letter-of-the-law judges and lawyers,
letter-of-the-law preachers,
letter-of-the-law doctors,
letter-of-the-law educators.

For all these heartless, psychopathic, go-by-the-book people are jailers in a psychotic halfway house on the way to hell.

Beware of the scribes and pharisees of modern times:

their cure is a sickness,
their law makes lawlessness
and their education drives out reason and
common sense.

As a light-loving plant thrives in the warmth of the sun, so are you meant to be a creature of the spiritual light. And through that inner illumination, God wordlessly suggests the way to go and grow.

But when through the life of knowledge your soul is cut off from the light, the darkness thing whispers the way.

* * * * *

Men's lives are made up
of many traumas,
and the memories of those
traumas form their thoughts.

And the spirit of that existence
is their god.

And the falling soul
is imprisoned in a rising
mist of thought, chained
to all the
compulsions of the flesh
until death releases him
to damnation.

And now I know why
I cannot remember
my childhood or my youth
or even yesterday;
because thanks be to
God I am made
of understanding stuff
like a flower is
made of sunlight,
part earth, part heaven,
and the Holy Spirit
has hidden Himself within
me and pulled around
Him the elements of
my being.

To this moment, at least,
I cannot remember
any trespass against me.
And now I know deeply what
God means when He

says if we forgive and forget
those who sin against us
then He forgets our
trespasses also.

And so, as I die to
this world, my memories
fade
and as knowledge passes
away, so does
guilt and sin.

In the Ever-Present,
I am becoming absent
minded, in that I
cannot remember like other
men do. I cannot
learn as others learn.
The willfulness and mindfulness of this
present world are passing
away as new knowledge
—understanding—comes.

I am forgetting now,
and remembering who I was
so as knowledge dies
so I die daily.

And as knowledge
and sin die,
death is consumed
in victory.

For in rejecting the
tree of knowledge I
leave behind sin
and the life of sin
that ends in death.

And so shall this
mortal put on immortality,
and this corruptible
become incorruptible
and the perishable
become imperishable.

I see you all from
afar, as through a
glass, struggling
like vipers in a pit
of slime.

And though I am in the
world I am
not of the world,
not in your world.

And there is a great
chasm between us
and you cannot come
across to touch
me where I am now.

For as Adam forgot
Truth in knowledge

and died through mortality,
so shall I live forgetting
knowledge and remembering
Truth eternally.

There, I see the
tree of everlasting life.

7 Evilution

Of all the fruits of the Garden ye may freely eat, except the fruit of the tree of the knowledge of good and evil...

A thought has no doubt flashed across your mind when observing a woman heavy with child: "I know what she's been up to," indicating that you feel the need to condemn or condone what the evidence points to. It is one thing to hear about babies being born, and yet another to witness it firsthand. It is pure shock to the psyche.

Now why should a perfectly normal, natural thing like having a baby affect us like that? Why should the way we arrive in the world be such an embarrassment? Could it just be that we are observing the way we come in the light of where we have fallen or descended from? Could it be that our natural origin shames us in the light of the other, more spiritual one? And could it be that the shock, the embarrassment, is an awakening?

It so happens that anything you do wrong has a similar effect. Guilt is experienced when the evidence of your sin awakens you to the conflict between what you have become and what you were before you sinned. What I am trying to say is that whatever sin is, it causes physical changes and that is what triggers conflict in the observer.

The sin-self is made up of evolved animal stuff, dependent upon external triggers. The more you add sin to sin (respond to ego-reassuring, reinforcing sources), the more you see a creature-life rise up in you. Now, if for some reason your creature-self were denied stimulation and isolated from the tease and temptation of pressure, then you might stop compensating and growing. It could make you feel as though you were dying, and the awakening to dreaded reality might also drive you mad.

Children, being first of nature, then of Spirit, need that natural stimulation to develop their animal selves; emotionally mature adults should not—they ought to be giving up the childish, self-seeking ego life. Only vain people are driven to emotional adventures after growing up.

If building your pride beyond its natural maturity is the bent of your vanity, or if you are under a compulsion to do so as a result of being pressured, you will then begin to experience the private hell of a sort of second fall. You observe yourself gradually devolving, becoming a beast-man, even as Adam fell to realize himself as an animal-man.

Every time you sin, a downward change occurs. If you will not or cannot yet see those pejorative devolutionary changes in yourself, then look at all the degenerate fools around you making your classic mistake, excusing what they are becoming in their prideful descent.

We have all inherited an animal identity by way of original sin, and that inheritance brings with it a natural embarrassment. Face it and live, or excuse it and keep on dying.

The way your ego reacts to self-conscious realization

when it reaches the zenith of its earthly animal-man development is a matter of life and death.

It happens to be the nature of pride never to admit fault as fault, and so it somehow pulls down the shades to the inner light, in which the sin-self is realized. This light, which allows you to see in depth spiritually, is from God, and this light holds the mysterious substance of our rebirth into His family.

Before that change can occur, pride must be humbled by realizing truth from the wordless language of conscience. We must suffer in the flesh, repeating (until we are dead, if necessary) the same sin of our common father, Adam. And his sin was to doubt truth, to fall, and to go on embracing lies to escape the guilt of failing to be a real man.

Just as Adam observed his bright-natured body change, so will you, by adding pride to pride and sin to sin, see your inherited animal-self become a beast-self.

At no matter what level of degeneration your ego finds itself, you smoke, drink and excuse the truth away. People tend to revel in the sweetness of their own foul smells. Be he homosexual, Nazi or drug addict, a wrong man invariably takes pride in what corruption has made of him and thus he promptly forgets the shame of sin. Every soul adapts and tries to feel at home in its own degenerate lifestyle.

To believe in man's progress through evolution is to believe in glory through sin, which is the same as believing that more rotten is more beautiful. We cling to what made us what we are to save us from seeing what we have become.

And no matter how low he sinks, a man can always

find (or make) a woman lower than himself. He always uses her to accept his failing self and to reinforce the lie, which is: that descent is ascent to glory. Hell's security depends on man's ego taking refuge in woman and giving his life in exchange for such a delusion. A woman represents the basis of life to a dying man. It is life—the life that leads to death. And through each shot of "life" reinforcement, a man can escape the reality of his false existence.

It has been said that behind every successful man stands a woman. But we always forget to ask about what is standing behind the woman.

Just as the violation of man came by way of the wrong use of woman, and just as his death-as-life is centered in the woman, so shall every fool one day see the author of his creation through sin. This creator is not God, but Satan himself. And he is our lord and savior in sin and beyond sinning. To the unaware, sin is an adventure, a doorway to enchantment. But when the sinner enters, he finds disenchantment; he discovers the awful truth—too late.

A successful appeal to the ego is responsible for all morbid physical changes. It was so in the beginning, and the proof of your origin is with you in every one of your experiences.

The vain, ambitious man demands that the embarrassing evidence of his change be worshipped. His mind is on sex continually. The worship of failing (sex) as virtue leads to lust, violence and death. How can a man interpret the deep meaning of failing if he revels in it? Lust then is where this failing is intensified as it is forgotten, and it is where the female soul mate becomes a cell mate. Man still marries for the wrong reason—for ego reinforcement—and women are still being employed in a

130

wrong way.

All change, good or bad, is centered in the soul of man, deep in his secret attitude. Through the pride of ambition came the change of the imperishable to the perishable. Having become death-centered through the woman's being, man's perpetuation by regeneration became perpetuation by generation. Today that heritage of pride is perpetuated through the process of sexual acceptance. If an addicted, lustful, woman-based man is denied that sexual support, he becomes resentful and violent. Sex and violence are relatives. They are energizers which maintain the male-ego status quo. A fearful or manipulative female can pacify or delay a man's rage through sex.

Through sex the man becomes ape and thinks that more ape is more man. Experiencing the ecstasy of escape, he can go on believing that his wrong existence is right, which is the same as doubting the truth. Doubting truth is original sin. Any reinforcement that makes wrong feel right, adds sin to sin, change to change, dependency to dependency and finally, rage to rage.

At best, sex represents death becoming new life. Sex is not necessarily sin; sex is the symptom, the outcrop, the *evidence* of original sin. And even though it is not our own sin, it nevertheless embarrasses us to tell our children where babies come from. Inherited guilt embarrasses us, and it embarrasses them. For the same reason (pride), our egos tend to accept death as a natural part of the good life. For if the ego were to stop to question death, it would also be forced to question the (sex) life which leads to personal death. Death (another symptom of failing, just as sex is) supports and justifies all the ways of pride.

When we are confronted with death, it is a shock to the system. Sex is too. That is why we glorify them—to glorify our failing. It all has to do with there being something wrong with the way we come into the world and go out. And so, when you see a baby born, there is a rude awakening, for birth reminds you of your own lowly beginning. And just as men need to have their manhood worshipped to overcome self-consciousness, so are women pleased to be exalted above disgust in their time—it just *has* to be a beautiful thing to have a baby. We are born in bed, we have sex in bed, and we die in bed. Our bed is our escape, our comfort and our refuge—even in the deepening sleep.

Sin is a transgression of the law (of the mind). Sin produces trauma, trauma produces change, and change is what you see after you sin. Threatened by the rude awakening, your ego can lose itself in the worship and the glorification of all observed changes. If the shock of sin can be made into a comfort and a friend, it then becomes the basis of the hang-up, while the sympathetic friend-in-need becomes the master manipulator of your weakness.

You are physically shocked by the truth of your animal, mortal origin when you observe a baby being born. And you stand at the dawning of the truth about your own beast emerging as you add every personal sin to the original one you inherit. Again, sin is to regard weakness as virtue, to give in to, pamper and indulge each particular failure of mind, body and soul, all the way from the embrace of sex to the embrace of death.

Sin translating into mortal flesh was originally due to a mysterious appeal to the soul. The temptation of sin led

132

to man's rejection of truth, to become that truth. The basic appeal was the power of *knowledge*. Now, no matter how shockingly rotten you become aspiring to knowledge, your hell-centered, glory-bound, emotionally self-righteous ego rarely, if ever, stops to realize its shame. Can you see how easy it is, without understanding, to turn the truth (concerning your evolving sensuality) around more to your liking with the rationale of *knowledge?* When knowledge was first experienced, it brought the shameful death-life, not glory. And now knowledge, through which evil made us what we are, rises to save us from realizing the truth of what we are.

If we deny the understanding of our common destiny, the ever-present and original viewpoint, then we are able to believe anything, especially the lie which justifies the evolving beast, because animal is all we see; and knowledge aids in this prejudice. Through knowledge we can also maintain the delusion that we are ascending to perfection rather than descending to chaos through imperfection because that is all we see and *prefer* to believe. Now, if we believe deeply *into* this idea of our ascending, we can arrive at the pleasing conclusion that there is no sin and no fault; and thus, in a subtle way, there is that renewed hope in old glory, new false courage in old false convictions, and the ancient covenant with death is strengthened.

The excuse always rises to rescue your ego, to explain the truth away after you have fallen. Rationalization is the collation of knowledge by the spirit of sin as a defense against the truth of failing. The spirit of rationalization makes sin out to be the true way, and makes the truth seem to be sinful.

The evil spirit of culture permits men to become immoral so as to allow itself to evolve through men while removing the repercussions of sin. And so it comes to pass that culture becomes everything as people become nothing.

Both in actual experience and in their fantasies, all egocentric men renew their ancient covenant with the devil, sensuality, delusion and death continuously without realizing it.

Without consciousness there could be no sin; the entire process of natural life would simply be unrolling from its beginning in God. But through consciousness comes the possibility of right or wrong, heaven or hell, through choice. Amongst God's creatures, consciousness exists in man alone. Only through him can life become reversed; only man can live backwards. ("Evil" is "live" spelled backwards.) Through choice comes failing, and through failing comes the compensating animal life which ends in death.

In its morbid, lie-loving state, the soul continues to seek its own truth through experience. To the egotist, experience is always an attempted escape from what is, into what is supposed to be (according to pride's plan). People even seek the "truth" of their glory and innocence in the experience of death itself, believing it to be the gateway to their reward in heaven.

Now death is a fact or scientific truth which sin has made real. The inevitability of death is the first manifestation of hell's truth which the ego is compelled to accept if it is to rationalize the glorious sin-self.

Our whole culture is based on a lie, and so when death appears through the lie, it also becomes a truth that we must accept. No longer creatures of faith, we are creatures of proof, of hard empirical evidence. How can the faithless deny the truth of death? It must be made to seem good if they are to preserve their God-image.

So by death do foolish and prideful men justify their lives. *The ego-life, then, is entirely based on the belief in death.* The sinful man's lot is to accept death; he must if his present lie-existence is to be made acceptable. Beware of the false-Christian doctrine that does not require change through repentance, that bases salvation in death rather than life.

Remember, the sex impulse in man represents the immortal soul dying to the true life and coming alive as a lower life-form that ends in death. Sex and death are related not only because of the biological replacement process, but also because foolish egotistical men feel most right and alive at the very moment they are being corrupted and destroyed.

I do, however, want you to realize that there are two kinds of sexual practices. While they both lead to death, it is the lustful, unnatural sexual relationship which leads to disease and a *premature* death. Lust must first give way to natural sex. For through lustful sex man fails to reflect upon the deeper meaning of sex in terms of failing, and so, through continually and stubbornly misusing the woman and reinforcing the sin-self, he adds sin to sin.

Let me set aside sex, birth and death for a moment and come back to that subject later. Let us continue unraveling the secrets of your attitude, by which you become entangled in a morbid sin-existence.

Just as the entire universe is built from only one building block complexing itself by adding one or more to itself continually, so is the sin-life built upon one single error repeating and adding to itself, ultimately being expressed in a multitude of troubles, sicknesses and tragedies.

Salvation is grasped only by realizing the correct sequence of beliefs, beginning with the willingness to understand the error of your ways, making the soul a fertile ground to receive grace.

You see, what we are really dealing with here is a process of deception through ever more complex ego-involvements with knowledge. That is why knowledge can never provide meaningful answers, only more anxieties, complexes and guilts.

The successful appeal of knowledge to the ego is a catalyst that awakens the sensual life. Every seed has its own special catalyst. Some seeds need a forest fire; others need to be carried in the bowels of animals before they can germinate. Knowledge germinates the sensual life of pride, and sexual acceptance sustains it.

If your attitude makes you compatible with knowledge, and if you are into knowledge, then understanding becomes your mortal enemy and knowledge is a refuge. If knowledge is your refuge, you are probably the kind of person who interprets guilt to mean that you simply haven't found or believed in your intrinsic goodness. You are not bad, you think, you simply haven't realized your perfection. And, as a devil's advocate, you will hold this kind of teaching up so other eager beavers will fall for it—they have, ever since Eden.

After the guilt of failing which knowledge brings, comes the need to make the guilt of sensual life seem innocent. If we can't be successful at least we can feel innocent. Most failures are preoccupied with being innocent. You can be God if you can only *feel* good.

The hypnotic trauma of a knowledge-experience can

lock you in one compartment of fantasy so that you don't see what lies in other areas of failing. You can justify just about anything because, once locked into your knowledge fantasy or ecstasy, you are egotistically sure, secure in the knowledge that you cannot perceive any contradictions. But it is only the willingness to see and face contradictions in yourself that would enable you to repent and to change.

Clearly, salvation hinges on a special kind of knowing and believing. Believing that birds fly is not the kind of belief that saves you; neither is knowing that we are descending or knowing that Jesus saves. The only belief that can save comes from being able to *realize the truth for yourself.*

Realization is salvation from knowledge. If you cannot realize for yourself, if the light of understanding does not shine, you will remain a victim of culture, satanically suggestible.

So, while believing the truth can save you from the sin of being suggestible to the lie, it only works when that truth is inwardly-realized.

Knowing through thinking can seem like understanding when it is not. Knowing through study-based thinking preserves the ego and makes us contemptuous, blind and proud. The rote study of true knowledge can *preserve* the ego nature when you are caught up in it, while understanding pains, awakens, humbles, and releases your soul from knowledge.

"Be still, and know that *I am* (not *you are*) God."

Truly, salvation comes by the soul leaving behind the refuge of the intellect and imagination. To realize that you know nothing is the beginning of true knowing.

Leaving behind the bedlam of suggestion where knowledge lies, you are drawn up and out of the machinery of your mind to an objective state of consciousness to *understand* God. Realization acts as a counterinfluence to suggestion and deception.

Realization saves.

Now if you are blessed to *realize* the sin of original failing by way of the additional evidence of your own sin and failing, you will stand at the threshold of the first truth for you. If a person cannot see that he needs salvation, he cannot draw it to him. In seeking salvation you will come to know that it does exist. You will be blessed to believe in life, instead of death. In spite of the overwhelming evidence of its inevitability, you will be empowered to disbelieve in the inevitability of death, a feat impossible to those without hope of life.

The truths you see at the dawning of reality are never shining truths, but negative ones. You see the truth about your rottenness, selfishness, hypocrisy and excuses. Above all, you see your willfulness struggling amid a sea of ideas, desperately trying to counter ideas and suggestions and trying to prove itself through all kinds of effort and decision-making.

If you cannot recognize the truth of your devolution, neither can you repent of it. You cannot resist the temptation to struggle. Repentance is the change of the soul in the light, by the light.

Be sure that your salvation ecstasy does not rise from the involvement with ideas and dogma. For any involvement with any *idea*, with the exquisite pleasure and hope in it, is sin.

And the ancient appeal to the ego of high-sounding

religious knowledge still comes from Satan through his elect who, with speeches and books, ensnare the unwary to feel piously innocent. Remember that knowledge of any kind can be a hypnotic religious experience through which we can escape. Remember also that the reference point of change and decay, and continued change and decay, revolves around the effect of the lie inherent in knowledge. The entire process of mortification hinges on the soul's embrace of some kind of lying promise to the ego. After that, the reinforcement of vanity through the worship of a procession of sin-symptoms acts as the trigger to evolution, the cycle of life and death.

What is it that turns you on? What do you want out of life? Whatever it is, there is a psychopath somewhere out there scanning your weaknesses in order to lead you through your particular aspiration. Whatever you secretly want to be, some psychopath will find it out and hold it up as a way to glory and greatness.

Once you have fallen into the pit of compulsion through knowledge, you have no free will left. All your choices and judgments henceforth come either out of feelings of obligation, or a special kind of rebellion *against* obligation.

Let us assume now that as a man you have a cozy relationship with a woman you have used to make your ego feel comfortable. You tend to feel guilty for using her and yet you become very uncomfortable giving her up. (And you might just want to give her up because you feel trapped.) Yet the very contemplation of breaking the relationship, of losing her, threatens you and makes you feel like the rotten egg you really are. You are in danger of waking up married out of need, guilt and obligation. Maybe to marry her is the right thing, maybe it is not. But the point here is this: if the decision to marry does not spring from a free will, the "choice" (obligation to relieve the guilt) enslaves you more. Although the desire to do the right and honorable thing may be there, it is hard to do it under the influence of obligation. Your choice narrows down to marriage without true agreement accompanied by seething resentment, or perhaps rebellion (now or later). You could try to break the spell by trying to find some fault in the woman, upsetting her into doing something wrong in order to get her to free you from her power.

Doubting the truth and not being committed to what is right leads to emotionalism, ego-support through emotion, enslavement through emotion, and degeneration through emotion. Another emotion—resentment—locks you in permanently and morbidly. And resentment is will struggling to free itself without understanding, avoiding understanding.

Remember, every decision is an exercise in pride-consciousness. And remember too that every scheming exercise in pride involves you more deeply with knowledge, which your ego needs to make decisions and to know itself as God while forgetting God and guilt. Scheming, worrying and decision-making can create so much guilt that they can make you very sick indeed.

So, whether you decide to do the right thing through obligation or the right or wrong thing through rebellion, you are damned either way. Every ego-based decision is an exercise in futility.

You are damned if you slide into marriage using the woman for comfort. But you are also damned (and discovering it) in your scheming to escape. And the guilt which you find in "freedom" can only be soothed by another bond of slavery. *People you have used can control you by withdrawing their support long enough to make you feel the pain of guilt that forces you to see things their way.* Then they embrace you with the kiss of death when you conform.

You must become free to make choices, or forever be manipulated in a compulsive decision-making process by the subtle power of suggestion under the tutelege of sin.

There is no true freedom without perfect integrity.

As soon as the power of realization begins to free your soul, you must be mindful of the lesson that the sin experience has taught you, which is:

> Never let people make you doubt yourself.
> For if you do, you will fall from grace
> and become emotional.
>
> Through your emotions you can now be
> *compelled* to doubt yourself and become
> even more emotional: a vicious circle.
>
> But how can you not doubt yourself?
>
> The answer is you must love the truth
> who honestly seek the answer to the
> riddle of existence.
>
> The original sin was to doubt the truth.
> Doubting truth reinforces the ego when it
> becomes wrong. Pleasure is a form of
> doubting truth—escaping.
>
> Whatever it is that can make us doubt

appeals to the need to be secure in our
wrong through emotion and through pleasure.

Hold fast, then, to what you are given to realize about yourself and others. Discern, don't judge. That is to say, don't mingle observation with emotion (good feelings or bad ones).

Never take advantage, and whenever you have the opportunity to do a kindness, do it. For if you fail to do what is right, or if you fall again into what is wrong, you become involved with evil again which you are forced to embrace in order to soothe a procession of pains and guilts. And you are also obligated to obey others for the sake of love and comfort, or suffer guilt from rejection.

But cheer up! The guilt you will feel is merely the conflict with God which has accumulated through pride seeking approval. Guilt is not bad. It is *you* who are bad. Realize you are wrong. Repent, and your sinful allegiances will sour and the guilt will vanish. If your ego wants acceptance, you cannot be yourself. When you realize the truth, the world will reject you and scoff at your new way in order to make you doubt.

Can you see how the fear of rejection sets you up for suggestion? Rejection, loss of friends and support, bares your soul to the Reality which you have selfishly betrayed. In order to avoid the pain of that, you are compelled to oblige others (ever so resentfully). Resentment is the energy of prideful judgment and resistance, and that itself leads to additional guilt. And the pain (the fear of truth, really) forces you to make up, to seek approval in order to soothe the guilt, or, as I said before, fiendishly find some fault in your manipulator to break the spell. But if you can't lick them you are forced to capitulate. And one day all the underground resentments which make you cling or jump out of the frying pan into other fires will surface as disease or weird forms of rebellion.

Again, let me emphasize that there is no perfect freedom from sin without perfect commitment to what is right in your heart. What is it you want in life? Do you want to be free from the selfishness of pride to do justice? Otherwise, it follows that you must become emotionally involved with people and things that gratify your growing needs and hungers, and that is not the freedom you think it to be.

Man clings, and woman encourages that clinging for the feeling of power. What you think you see is a man loving a woman, but what is really happening is a man escaping from guilt, recharging his fallen existence by clinging to the God-mother of his fallen existence. A penis-worshipping woman represents life to the dying male ego. But the life he finds in her is the animal life that leads to death.

Sex hang-ups lead to pain, and pain leads to needing more women, wine and song to take the pain away. All hang-ups have the same sensual, sexual theme: a deepening, comforting involvement with objects of corruption. A man cannot give up what it is he loves because when he clings he thinks that he is getting something out of it (when it is really killing him). Clinging to what fulfills through craving makes you forget the truth. Addiction to anything is like a perverted love for God; it draws you deeper and deeper into slavery, even as love of God binds you ever closer to Him in obedient service. The mystery of your fascination with evil has to do with its recognition and subtle acceptance of your fallen nature, and with its stroking of all your symptoms of pride.

No man can decide to give up alcohol or drugs, because he is not free to decide anything. His pride needs those things to reinforce his ego-life and to help him escape the shame and guilt of failing to face reality. He becomes less of a man in every embrace, and then he promptly craves it even more because he is afraid to see how much more degenerate he has become.

A man cannot stop embracing what is killing him. For even if his pain and need do eventually make him realize that he is a slave, his resentment against the truth of it drives him further into slavery.

What I am trying to emphasize here is that all decisions made in the fallen state lead to more corruption and frustration. And every conformity or rebellion turns the wheel of nature and the cycle of life and death. You struggle only when you have fallen into the current of mind and emotion. And there is less current, and eventually no current at all, as you see clearly and as you gain the strength which comes from knowing deeply.

All decisions lead to conflict, and the guilt of deciding always makes the comforting embrace of any form of temptation more attractive. All decisions are both prideful and compulsive. Your love is compulsive and so is your rebellion against it when you realize it has enslaved you. You are damned by *any* decision—whether you should drink or not, whether or not you go to a doctor—because such decisions involve making judgments based on knowledge; and every judgment is an exercise of ego futility that leads to more guilt and pain which you try to resolve with more decisions.

Rebellion against the enslavement of one comfort only leads you to comfort at the hands of another enslaver. No matter how many times you rebel, you will be conforming to the will of hell.

All decisions are an exercise in futility and lead to guilt. All decisions favor the hell that has teased you, pressured you and made you what you are. For you are *never* morally free to make a true choice until you find the secret way out through meditation.

You will this, and you will that, in order to make something happen. Then it backfires and you become sick and guilty. Driven by resentment, you seek to remedy it as if you were trying to prove you had some divine power to change things for the better. No matter what you do, it is based on the same theme: the will to power, and the will to get rid of pain, guilts and sickness that come from the will to power. And *every* exercise of will-as-God causes more conflict with God.

Most people don't want to be responsible to what is higher than themselves. They are pleased to mistake the voice of the unconscious for their own conscience.

The voice which reflects back up from the depths of our minds, brings up with it the kind of answers that glorify and justify the ego in all its selfish endeavors. The spirit behind those words of knowledge and guidance is Satan himself.

Downward, beyond the borders of the subconscious mind, lurks the serpent of old with knowledge to swell our pride, to mislead, to excuse, and to force us to indulge and revel in our evolving passions.

That voice in you is the spirit which also lives through others. It is in all the foolish females who allow you men the unlawful, unbridled embrace of their bodies for the power they secretly know they will have over you as they weaken you by reinforcing your ego.

And for every one of you who is lost in his own head there is persuasive, permissiveness-evolving psychology, a false logic that always convinces you to reach longingly to the spirit of your corruption. And it, in you, draws you to it in them.

Blessed is he who does not trust the echoes of his deceiving mind, and realizes the truth.

Does not the Scripture say, "Incline not to thine own understanding"? What is meant, of course, is: don't look away from truth to knowledge. Don't look faithlessly toward intellectual answers, for you will surely be deceived.

But if deception is what you want, expect the evil force to rise through knowledge with hypnotic suggestion as if you had crowed sweetly for his presence. If the light is not your reality, imagination becomes your reality, and that reality is controlled by the spirit that tempted you there.

And when he has thoroughly corrupted your soul, you will hear that voice of voices that you thought to be your good conscience speaking vile things, cursing God, playing strange games with your mind. And he will severely torment your thinking soul. For it will never be you who thinks, but evil thinking through you.

Now the voices in your head can force you to make the most absurd mental decisions. Each silly antic you are compelled to perform in order to appease the painful mental tease becomes the basis of more agony and resentment. For the need to exercise your ego represents a need to find righteousness, even as God is seen to be righteous by what He decides. But through guilt, your judgments in life eventually become limited to absurd head-games. You are tormented to death by the need to make decisions in order to escape the guilt of making decisions.

The voice might say to you, for instance, "Don't wash, because if you are clean you will be like God and that is agony." So you may stay dirty, becoming trapped into another discomforting ego-decision by your efforts to be comfortable, and thus accumulating another guilt. Perhaps you might hear a tormenting noise when you breathe which stops when you stop breathing. Deciding to control that could kill you. And the same kind of thing may happen with food. Since overeating is an ego trip and produces guilt, you could decide that not eating will take the agony and pride away (and that is more pride and guilt).

Remember that any exercise of decision carries with it the false implication that we are free creatures determining our own destiny. But in our stubborn pride, our fate is to go on deciding compulsively, blindly choosing death in our willful deciding—suffering agony through each ecstasy of choice. Every exercise of ego through knowledge judgments is an exercise in prideful futility, and all the devils outside you and inside you know that. Once you decide to decide, you can't stop making decisions, because if you do, you will see that you are dead in that life of deciding.

Anyway, it is no longer you who decides anything. It is Satan who tempts you to decide all things. *For through all your struggles and acts of will, the will of hell is actuated.* In other words, everything you do is wrong and harmful.

You are unconsciously seeking divinity through every choice and you cannot resist the temptation to escape the truth and prove yourself through this exercise until the day you are willing to realize the supreme folly of it all.

If it be Thy will, O Lord, let this reader realize Thy truth, and save him from the sin of saving himself from sin.

8 The Passion and the Poison

What you are about to read cuts as close to the nerve center of all human misery as can be conveyed through words. Each person who reads this will identify with it as he flashes upon his own experiences. Even though you may not have read this anywhere else, you will mysteriously and instantly recognize what is said, proving the omniscience and ever-presence of truth. And it just may be that the power of it will overwhelm you and save you from your suffering.

Unfolding before your eyes in just a few pages is the root of all sickness and suffering—even war itself. And no matter how many times you read the same words, they will take on new meaning, new depth, encompass more relationships and expose more human folly.

It is too much to expect words alone to express all I want to convey. Your own mind must go beyond the horizon of the written word. And if it please God, the Spirit will witness and interpret in such a way as to free you once and for all from your enslavement and compulsions.

There is in all of us an unhealthy need for something or someone to stimulate and excite us, to make us feel alive and happy. As we grow older and more corrupt, ordinary stimulation from people ceases to be enough and we look down to the world of beasts and drugs (and other poisons) to turn us on or off. There is no depth to which a depraved man will not sink for escape and for excitement. To escape (through excitement) is to lose awareness, and to lose awareness so as to relieve guilt is to let something unspeakably evil enter, take up residence, and act as a parasite on one's soul. We cling to what corrupts us, and as we draw security from it, it draws life from us.

At this point, that thing in you may want to make you drop this book as if it were a hot coal, as if the spirit expressed in this book were a demon. But if you are blessed, the real you—now a prisoner of the passion and the poison—beckons you to read on. No matter what the pain or the price you must pay, in a wordless way it says, read on.

As every slave has a need, so every master has a need to be needed. In his psychotic state, the victim's need cries out to be fulfilled by the reinforcing love of the tyrant who created it.

NEED comes from a dying, guilty, falling soul crying for identity and for life. It is a baby hell sucking at the bosom of the parent hell, which, in turn, lives through its child.

TENSION is the life force that gratifies such a need. And tension is generated in the familiar presence of that temptation which created the creature and its need. Every (traumatic) experience which gratifies creature-need is itself another corruption. Each experience provides, through tension, certain ingredients for egocentric development such as: identity reinforcement, apparent life, growth, false innocence, distraction and pleasure.

150

The very presence of a person, animal or object can generate just enough tension to keep the mind distracted from its guilt. The addict cannot live without a stimulating, lowly external presence of some kind, even if it is only a pet dog.

A guileful female delights in teasing and irritating and then rewarding a man's failing with her body. Men derive pleasure from the distraction of a female tease, and they are also very happy and grateful to be released from such sexually-induced tensions. Men's greatest ego-pleasure lies in having their failings stroked as if they were virtues and their compulsions rewarded as if they were loyalties.

The less tension (pain) there is, the less relief (pleasure) there can be. *Without the original tease, and then the release from it, there can be no (release of) pleasure.* Bear this fact in mind; it is most important:

IF YOU DO NOT TEASE YOURSELF ON THE ONE HAND, YOU WILL NOT BE A SLAVE OF PLEASURE ON THE OTHER.

Too much tension evolves to become compulsion in terms of sex and violence. A climax in either behavioral extreme brings release from pain, while actually serving the will and purpose of the provocateur behind the tease.

The temptress or rabble-rouser first provokes, with a wiggle, or with a hint of meanness. Then he or she offers a release, an avenue of expression in terms of sex or violence. He or she has the power first to cause the tension (guilt-release) we need, and later to relieve that excessive tension, subtly rewarding the errant behavior. Both the need to be excited and the need for relief from excessive tension will appear to be love for the provocateur. Some people actually seek terrible cruelty in order to feel teased, loved and fulfilled.

We become tense because of ego-need and guilt. When we discover that tension feels good, in that it releases us from guilt and boredom, we greedily gobble up more to stay ahead of the guilt of that. It is like eating something so good you can't stop until the pain comes. Then you get to feel good again by relieving your indigestion with seltzer water and starting all over again.

Our human need for one another and for "life and love" is really a misdirected need for God. Our cry of need arouses the false compassion of those who have a need to be needed.

Again, the driving force behind the need to be aroused is the desire to escape and to ease the anguish of guilt. We need tension to pull us away from anxiety.

Our psychopathic counterparts, who have a need to arouse and please, are also driven by guilt, which they are able to forget as they bloat up with power sucked from their victims.

Breaking down need into two unconscious drives, we see the following:

1) a need to escape from guilt, which leads to
2) the emotions and tensions of animal life.

The more guilt you have, the more spiritually dead you are. The tensions which you think of as "life," which help you to forget that guilt, now become more attractive. You think you are becoming more at the very moment that you are being destroyed, literally eaten alive. And rising to the ego-need to escape into the false life and false innocence is that tension: tension by way of sex, and tension induced by impatience. Tension has a constant value no matter whether it involves a sexual or violent partner-source.

The basis of tension is irritation, and in turn the basis of irritation is wickedness. According to the particular requirement of the moment, there is need either for sexual irritation, or aggravation by way of hostility. Eagerly gobbling up that tension leads to the problem of easing the pain of it. Tension releases you from guilt one way, as it produces guilt in another. The relief of guilt produced by sexual tensions, tease and ultimate pleasure in climax, causes more guilt. And that can lead to relief through resentment-tease with expression in violence.

Your need to be irritated and sexually aroused could express itself against those weaker than yourself. You might go to see a chorus line and then go home and take it out on your wife. The same holds true with violence. You need a big wickedness to serve the same secret need. Rabble-rousing and rallying armies against a common enemy is a Satan-principle of war.

The sexual provocation which you so often require can even be, and often is, *cultivated* in your own children. The need for excitement (love or hate) can cause a father to degrade his daughter through encouraging her to arouse him sexually in order to serve his ego. Mother, on the other hand, often coaxes the violence of her son to serve her need for tension—hence the morbid chain, the heritage of Original Sin. Reading the wrong meaning into the natural playfulness of little children is yet another way of creating the tension you need. That tension produces the familiar impatience, ending in violence in your own home.

Need, and the need to be needed, perpetuate an unholy dependency upon material things and the wicked, supportive services of the flesh. We are like drunks holding one another up. Between sexual intrigue and violence, we build a life on a foundation of nothing but dead bones and deceit.

You can love-hate just about anything. You can hate (resent) something for energy value, and you can turn around and love it for a release. You can be very close to your mother, your husband or your work. The process underlying addiction to almost everything involves the resentment factor first, and the release factor in work, sex and violence second.

I cannot say it enough times: Your fascination with anything begins with its excitement or resentment value, which gives you the tension-energy, the libido or drive your fallen ego needs to function, survive and "express itself."

And the release factor—the sex, violence and hard work—can follow so closely on the heels of the resentment/excitement factor that one may never observe the underlying resentment at all. We notice only our "righteous" rage, or our love and devotion to our work or irritating, demanding partner, wife or boss.

To describe our involvement with anything, we often use the word "into." We are into this or into that. And part of the pleasure of the hate-love or love-hate-love relationship is the tease-escape into something. So, people lose themselves *into* whatever or whomever it is. Consequently, your reaction to what you are aroused by, and lost in, is not a normal one. It is an *over*-reaction, a trauma that lowers the consciousness and triggers the evolutionary (devolutionary) process of identity.

Becoming more of an animal and demon is the only

"more" there is for us in our pride. It is growth through an unholy escape into an animal self. But losing ourselves in identifying with the body is never enough. We go on to lose ourselves in people, places and things, with guilt following like a hound from heaven.

Just as the body has an animal identity, the soul, too, must have an identity. Guilt and emptiness drive us to cling to the spirit of temptation for its identity, for what appears to be life and growth. Do you see now that the main value behind both pleasure and pain is partly escape, partly animal growth and partly identity?

The less tease-reaction tension, the less pleasure. To find less "happiness" through experience means that you are either reacting less and developing true love for people through love of God, or, it means that pleasure is causing you so much pain (damage to the body through abuse) that the guilt is disenchanting you.

Now when you are too guilty to enjoy pleasure any more, you are set up to enjoy pure pain. You may feel that you are not worthy to enjoy pleasure or the good life, so you give it all up for pain. The tension caused by resenting the torment of cruelty or harsh circumstance, is the means by which we originally produced feelings of life (and release of guilt). We can revel in self-inflicted punishment. But remember, we are not really punishing ourselves—we are *enjoying* ourselves, attempting to relieve guilt through tease and judgment.

Strange how we can find pleasure in pain, and how the intensity of the pleasure can be increased with the intensity of the tension—even when it makes us dangerously ill (we can resent that too). Pain distracts, just as pleasure does. A physical discomfort distracts and thus relieves a

155

severe spiritual discomfort—that is how we come to enjoy pain. Since pleasure is the release of pain, it does not have as much substance and permanence as pain. Pain is a more powerful form of guilt-relief.

The basis of any false happiness is the avoidance of the painful encounter with God. We think we *are* God, right in our wrong being. We are like naughty kids, taking secret ego-pleasure in eating the forbidden fruit in Papa's pantry.

And like guilty little children, you find that you are fidgety and it is hard to sit still when you meditate.

You seem to be bored, as reality and anxiety catch up with you.

You have the impulse to run.

You think about things you can do to get away. And thoughts rise about what to do.

Your bones cry out for irritation. You see rage rising.

Whatever it is you think about in those moments, it is always for its escape excitement, its relief value in terms of tease, sex and violence.

See now how every decision you make is self-serving. You opt for what will provide tension (false life) and, later, the relief of tension. You buy things for their excitement value, and although you may buy the right things, you use them in the wrong way. You involve yourself in an unholy manner with others for that vitalizing escape, for tension and for the release of tension wherein lies more pain. And you promptly find yourself enslaved to one thing and then to another.

All decisions embrace the enslaving services of some evil or other because every sinner clings to what teases and pleases. Loving evil (clinging in need) and hating evil, *you* eventually *become* that evil, and nothing good ever comes through.

I have said that the tension which the mortal soul *demands* can be produced by either of two irritants: sex irritation and/or hostility irritation. But in order to continue to irritate, something must be more and more wrong with the person doing the irritating. Honest people simply will not rise to the role. Evil alone can promote the growth of the ego and the animal.

None of us could stand it one moment were the world to become perfect. If the world were perfect, our tease-tainted souls would be bared to the inner light. Our present existence, you see, is rooted in the need for tease. Wickedness is exciting. Wickedness excites when it lies and makes us feel good, and we also delight in our hatred of it. Either way, it distracts from guilt, and makes us feel alive in the deadness of our sin through pleasure and pain.

Men fall for guileful females who have the power to irritate sexually. Falling men feel alive in their presence and right in their wrong. Such women close the trap on fools by accepting their fall. The lure of the female's exitement is the bait set for weakness, and her body closes the trap.

Cruelty often translates into sexual desire. Women know that men are good for a little extra "love" after they are tempted with an aggravation. The reason why aggravation arouses a man sexually is because any form of ego failing tends to express itself in sexual terms. The first sensual expression of sin is sex. So when a female opens herself to accept a man, she is, in fact, supporting what is wrong with that man. And they don't know what they are getting into.

Now there are actually two faces of temptation. There is stress-trauma and comfort-trauma. Both revolve around a temptation theme. One temptation teases and releases energy, and the other draws the tension off. What seduced you and made you what you are, will rise to comfort you as you are. And too much comfort can suck you dry. As you roll over in pleasure like a dog being scratched, you meekly, and with great pleasure, surrender your life to what despises you and holds you in the greatest contempt. You are corrupted when you are teased and you are again corrupted when you are comforted. Any comfort, being itself a temptation, can bring out the sexual desire for the comforter.

The comfort-trauma, then, drains off excess energy, relieving pain and giving pleasure by contrast. But your life drains away. Because that kind of pleasure is the only happiness the sinner has, the experience becomes a reward for weakness as well as an encouragement to go on sinning (that is, to go on being prideful and ambitious).

To have pleasure, one must also have pain. The sin of pleasure sets us up for more pain, and pain sets us up for even greater pleasure, and between the two, we think all is well in ego never-never land. The more wrong a person is, the more right he thinks he is when he relieves the pain.

It is mainly resentment that sets you up for the ultimate surrender to love-comfort. Hostility, you see, is a form of obedience in that it is basically an ego-need being served by irritation. Have you ever heard of the phenomenon of fighting and making up in bed? We can take *any* form of pressure for its temptation-irritation value and then we give in to the pressure-source for the reward of relief and acceptance. We let ourselves see the wickedness just long enough to serve us a judgment value, and soon it begins to look good to us again.

How many times have you come home from a vacation more tired than when you left? Could the reason be that you sought an ego reward, a comfort (in an escape from the tension of life in general) from your vacation experience? Those guileful exploiters at vacationland drained you of money and emotion because that is their function and their livelihood. Massage parlors offer the same sort of service. There is a special breed of parasite which exists to drain you of excess energy and guilt money, and these psychopaths come offering their services in many forms. Personally, I never enjoyed wasting money on a vacation. While other people seemed oblivious to the contempt and money lust of their hosts, I could see what kind of leeches and hypocrites were providing for my "comfort."

Remember the rule again: being irritated and being comforted both necessitate obedience and surrender. You obey when you respond with hostility, and that sets you up for the need to surrender to the comfort, another obedience and sin.

Many diseases are caused by draining nerve energy from your body. Leukemia is one, and asthma is another.

The sinning populace is like a herd of goats which exists for the parasite-elite. They feed you hay and take your milk and eat your babies—that is, if you don't devour your own children first.

Once you begin to respond, the reins of your mind are handed over to that which tempted you originally. Your guilt and need addict you to the emotion which all tempters can cleverly generate in you. Your baby hell calls to the parent hell, and up it comes to comfort your conflict with its vampirish love. For this reason, it would be wise never to sleep cuddling one another all night. Husband and wife must find the natural spiritual restoration which comes through proper meditation and sleep.

Animals have two natural triggers which we know as hate and love. But for man to be turned on that way is sub-natural. What made him an animal now keeps him securely lost in his animal self.

The spiritually dying seek reassurances through the only life they know—the animal life, which is triggered when stroked by some pleasing wickedness. Failing to find the source of God's life-fulfillment and inner warmth, something must be employed to serve, develop, tease and sustain the ego-animal life.

There is the animal life which comes from motion, and there is that true spiritual life which comes from the stillness. The life from the stillness does not answer to the pressures of the world, and it projects a beautiful environment for your body to perfect itself in. The life which comes from emotion projects an ugly world for you to grub in and die in.

The life from the world shouts for and projects its need to be irritated, and something shoots out of you into others and charges them to play the devil's role you need in terms of sex and violence. And all the while, as your needs are being serviced, you are being corrupted and enslaved. To be carnally minded is death. And through your preoccupation, involvements and identification with excitement sources, you become separated from the life of stillness and you become mortally *dependent* upon the evils and upsets of the world. Sinners, then, draw psychopaths out of hell to serve (rule) them.

Be very still now. Observe your bones aching, crying out for life, and let the irritation pass.

Do you see two opposing forms of need here? One of them is to *run* from the stillness through sex or rage energy which your ego calls up. But the other, true need is to *be* still, so that you may experience the kind of energy that is called up through patience.

Every fallen ego fulfills its need for tension through resentment or irritation. Guilty people always throw a monkey wrench into the works to stir up any peaceful relationship. We all tend to be threatened by too much peace. With too much peace, your animal-self begins to die and your ego is tormented before its time. Your pride is threatened by the divine peace, by the truth, the original life which comes from stillness.

If you wish to find the spiritual life and breath, you must be still and let the need for irritation pass. You must give up objects of escape and stimulation. Let the need to reach for something or someone pass. Let the need to flee from the moment, into fantasy, pass.

Don't run from the shame, the purging, redeeming pain of the stillness, to fulfill your own ego-life needs in some kind of excitement or activity. You have done it all before. Remember how it made matters worse?

Observe, then, your need to be irritated. Observe yourself thinking up fantasies and distractions, something exciting to do, from someone to sex to someone to be angry with.

Let that moment pass, and lo! Discover a new reward:

the warmth, the comfort of true life which comes welling up through the stillness.

The motion which springs from such rest revolves about the will of God.

The motion which comes from emotion is nothing more than a willful escape which serves Satan's will and purpose on earth as it is in hell. But don't struggle against your compulsion to run, lest you become more willfully and emotionally involved. You can never free yourself. Only the truth will make you free. Realizing this will help you find peace and rest.

The divine rest leads back to the reward of motion (life) through that true rest. And any motion which comes from that rest produces a co-creative life without fear, and without conflict.

Without the emotions of love and hate there is no sustained false hope, no ego life and breath. Therefore, if you can let the need to be aroused pass, you will not be addicted to its relief!

Do you see how it is? The *tension* we need to release us from guilt and deadness on one hand leads around to the clinging, selfish *affection* for that which releases us from the guilt of that false life on the other hand. Alas, the drain of love lays bare our guilt again, and guilt sets up the need to blame and the need for the tease of violence. Do you see why, for example, a drunk needs a good upset? Otherwise, he cannot enjoy the relief of his drinking. It is the "no pain, no pleasure" principle. Evil provides pain and evil provides pleasure. Pleasure is the only happiness of a sinner, and through it he meekly surrenders his soul.

So now do you see why egocentric men delight in the

162

very tensions and emotions they ought to be mastering? The guilt rising from reacting to the evil stress they need drives them to embrace the evil stress of comfort, and the evil comfort of stress, with greater and greater intensity. Through the stress of sex or violence does the heart of man give out, and does he die before his time. And through excessive comfort is his soul punctured, and his brains, bones and sinew ooze out, his blood vessels collapse.

While a male tends to give up energy as he is relieved, a female tends to bloat up with power that is not good for her to have. And so guileful females, like wicked politicians, can learn to relieve the guilt of power through drinking in more power, either through the tease temptation of "easy virtue" or through being bitchy, witchy, and aggravating the life out of everyone around them.

When men find true love from the stillness, they stop giving power to women and politicians; they also cease holding high the whores of art, religion and science. And when the Satan principle has been exposed, and when those superstars fall from the heavens like ripe figs off a shaken tree, then shall the Kingdom of God come.

The total lesson here is that you must realize the danger of the excitement of your subnormal relationships and shrink from them completely. Then you must look at your more natural needs and not escape into them anymore. For instance, don't make more out of sex and food than is honestly there. For it is the wrong relationship with your more natural needs that intensifies the pleasure of normal feelings, and that abuse will lead to sickness and guilt, and to seeking the services of the more bizarre helpers.

You can never be free of anything until you relate to it

properly. Your work, your marriage, your food, were never meant to enslave, nor were friendship or material things. But they do, because you use them to get high. If you promote things and people to play the tempter's role, you change their nature, drawing up evil through them to serve you. And that evil which you embrace in them contemptuously enslaves your soul. Alas, you will enjoy your resentment in servitude. For your servitude is required to support the wickedness you *need* to provide you with hate and love.

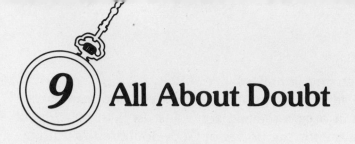

9 All About Doubt

Emotion is the natural survival mechanism against any threat. Lie detectors work by measuring electrical impulses which indicate the individual's response to attempts to get at the truth. From this evidence we can conclude that in man, emotional responses arise not only in reply to danger, but also in defense against the truth (which is seen as a threat to the ego).

While emotion is indeed a survival mechanism for animals and perhaps for plants, in man it takes on a special significance: emotion is an *ego-defense* animal survival-mechanism.

The guilty fear being found out. The corrupted soul shields itself with lies and excuses to avoid being exposed. *It takes energy to reject reality and accept the lie, and that energy manifests as emotion.* It also takes energy to reject and defend oneself against evil, and that is the divine energy of grace—love.

At the very heart of the emotional rejection of truth is a mysterious doubt. The ego (which is trying to survive as an ego) must doubt truth to keep from being humiliated. Doubt, you see, being the opposite of faith, has its own, animal energy (emotion).

From faith in the truth comes love, and love is the defense of a light-seeking soul. Just as faith joins us to and draws upon the power of God, doubt repels truth by drawing upon the power of stress—that emotional-assist factor provided by evil. Emotion is the primitive, driving force of pride, as love is the divine energy of humility.

Love is the response of faith, which appears as non-response in the face of the stress of temptation. Whosoever is pure and truthful, is calm.

Faith is a loving response to the Master. Doubt, on the other hand, is a defensive response to a different master-presence. Doubt can always be counted upon to produce emotion and, conversely, emotion to produce doubt. In other words, emotion can comfort and keep you blinded to reality. I am, of course, loading you up for what is to follow in this text.

Notice how people become angry when you face them with their faults. And notice, too, how their egos become excited by flattery. Belief in a lie supports their *doubt* of the truth that they are wrong, and that wrong belief excites them.

It is the nature of a sinner to find false salvation, a sort of bizarre security through doubt. And this, my dear reader, is the central theme of all the suffering, disease, war and misery that ever was or ever will be.

Emotion has long been the friend of the guilty. Like it or not, we all are polarized in favor of those who can generate emotions (doubt), thereby relieving us of our anxiety (temporarily).

The main reason why you cannot control your emotions is that your ego needs those very emotions for its defense and security—not so much against dangers, but more so for the survival of your ego life and breath against the light of reality. A veiling mist of emotion protects your ego against guilt feelings and provides the power with which to conquer, to move and have a vile, prideful, ambitious being.

People use both imaginary and real danger (often situations they have brought upon themselves through folly) to generate the emotion they need to protect their egos from the light.

Poisons such as alcohol, tobacco and other drugs are also employed to cause those emotional, defensive responses. The more we sin, the deader we realize we are, and the more the ego responds to this threat with the stress of drug-induced life-stimulus. Poisons inhaled, injected or eaten, trigger emotional responses that create the illusion of life and relief. We drink to forget, to escape—to feel good and to feel free. Escape from what? Forget what? Feel free from what?

Bullfighting, sports events, wild parties and rowdy, boisterous behavior—just about any excitement that can arouse emotion can relieve the tension of the soul's conflict with reality. Those wild whoops of delight which emotions bring, come from sick men and women discovering new hope and faith in their foolish ways. Anything which produces emotion can make us stand up and cheer, for the spirit of emotion is the champion of our prideful cause.

For example, the guilt of a son who has betrayed his father's trust can make him fear and flee the presence of his father. So out he goes into the world, currying favor with friends to get them to support him and make him feel confident about what he is. Through lies and adventures he is able to find comfort in emotions and, through emotions, that false faith in himself.

False faith is doubt of truth, and doubt preserves the ego's status quo through emotionality. It is this saving face, this doing exciting things for love and reassurance, that forms the basis of addiction. All any true son need do is come back to the true Father and say, "Father, I have wronged you." But to believe in itself, to survive pridefully as God, the ego which is wrong (for playing God) must forever doubt that it is wrong. And so that need drives one away from God and draws upon temptation.

There are two kinds of doubt—one when you are wrong, and another when you are right. And in a thousand, thousand ways friend Satan tries to rob you of repentance by his exciting emotional reassurances, his intrigues, playing one kind of doubt against the other.

Having faith in God was once centered in the *choice:* to believe or to doubt Him. Now that salvation through Christ has come, man could be saved from Adam's fatal choice if he could only stop being so *emotionally* defensive against realizing the error of his ways.

Choice is the prerogative of God. Therefore, once we aspire to become a god in our own eyes through choosing, we are obliged to maintain a false faith in ourselves through choosing. Choosing now becomes a compulsion and is tied in with struggle, doubt and emotion. If you can realize this, then the truth which you must believe *into,* so as to doubt the lie, is dawning. Once you see how much you need saving from making decisions and doubting, perhaps that realization alone will save you from all those faithless, emotional struggles to save yourself.

This chapter is about the relationship between the agony of doubt, the futility of decision making, and your emotions.

Uncontrolled emotions arise as faith disintegrates (into the intellectual process). Your faith and confidence are most often destroyed through pressure-education. Allow me to frame the principle, and say it again in many different ways.

Any ego weakness (lack of faith in or lack of commitment to what you intuitively know is right in your heart) causes you to become a victim of suggestive persuasion through doubt and emotion. Emotion rises as faith fails. Love is the energy of faith, just as emotion is the energy of pride through doubt.

So, as you fall away from the ground of your being through a successful appeal to your ego, you become a victim of your emotions through doubt. You feel pressure now because you have fallen from faith to become subject to pressure, which, in turn, makes you a creature of hypnotic suggestion through your emotional responses. Lost now in the intellectual process through your emotions (which you need), your ego is chained to the changing mood of circumstance and the power of suggestion as whispered by Satan.

As a victim of emotion through pressure, your mind is programmed and force-educated. No longer are you in control of what you accept or reject. Your beliefs are shaped. Your beliefs are led. You see people everywhere clinging to their silly cultures and their seducers, to whatever it is they have been brought up to believe. Why is this? They are all cooperating now to stay ahead of the guilt of having been converted to foolishness.

Whether you like it or not, the emotional state you find yourself in sets you up to be challenged toward prideful achievements. Before the fall to temptation, an ego appeal to your greed for power and glory was all that was needed to string you along. But now you are doubting, deciding and falling compulsively. Through original sin your ego is *inherently* suggestible through your emotions, and you respond to challenges for the same reason. Your ego weakness may take either of the following forms:

1) You suffer from stubborn pride: here you willfully continue the heritage of pride, ambition and irresponsibility, in which case you revel in dehumanizing emotions that help you to doubt what is true and which liberate you from conscience and revive your wrong-as-right existence, or

2) You are not ambitious, but your emotion chains you to the way of pride (sin) anyway, and prevents you from coming up to the state of grace. In this case, you find yourself driven toward prideful achievement through suggestibility and your soul's subjectivity to wicked challenges and pressures. Even though you sin as the result of compulsion, it still produces a guilt which makes you resentful and defensive. And this resentment, which makes you serve others for approval, makes you more an enemy of reality.

Humanly speaking, it is absolutely impossible by effort of will to shake free of believing in or struggling against whatever the system wants you to be or to accept. For salvation to occur you must become objective to the love-hate process and, most importantly, you must welcome, rather than resent, the realization of what is wrong. You must be willing to set aside malice and selfish ego-advantages in order for the light to enter your life.

Let me repeat the basic theme again: the basis of sin is pride.

Remember that the ally of pride is doubt, and the energy of pride through doubt is emotion. And sin, which the soul experiences through emotion, makes you crave more emotion (energy) to maintain your belief in yourself and to escape from guilt. The escape is tantamount to a rejection of reality and hence it is another fall, bringing with it the need for even more emotion to escape again and again. Although doubt is the cause of falling (to emotion), it is emotion which can be counted on to perpetuate and maintain pride through doubt. Doubt causes the ego to fall, but if we can then doubt that we have fallen, pride is maintained. Doubt makes us emotional (ego-secure), while emotion, in turn, sustains doubt. *In this manner, people can make you doubt your true self through upsetting you.*

Allow me to reiterate: emotions which we can't (or won't) control provide the willful, guilty ego with a sense of relief through liberating it from conscience by their power to make us doubt.

There is a single theme here, variations of which are legion and which run through the fabric of our entire being, and that particular theme is the strange need to energize a false sense of well-being through doubt, emotions and the people and circumstances which produce them. We need to employ someone to generate that emotion to make our deadness feel alive, our wrongs seem right. For without emotions, good or bad, we awaken to the "cruel" truth before we are ready to accept it. Ironically, if only to doubt God, we draw tragedy to ourselves.

The vain and the treacherous feel what they call a

"beautifying" release through their emotions. Realizing this error, it would be wise for you to take stock of your emotions and be careful never to revel in them as those people do. Be ever careful not to fall to any tempting morsel of aggravation. Because to the degree that you can resist the sweetmeats of those tempting love/hate offerings from the beautifully wicked or the wickedly wicked who generate emotion in you, to that degree will emotion subside. With every successful encounter, the power of hypnotic suggestion diminishes. Your compulsive thoughts, based on emotion, will melt away and you will be freer. Understanding will emerge to form the basis of the faith and strength which comes from such knowing. Understanding, which once made you cringe and reach for the emotional escape, will now save you from the emotional life—and from sin.

Do you see how you have become addicted to evil pressures? It is because your guilty ego, together with your pride, craved pressure in order to provide a basis of emotion for false confidence (doubt of truth) into which your ego escaped for its adventure and its sense of life.

Your two weaknesses, then, are (1) lack of faith in your higher self, in the perfect justice of good, and (2) the emotions which rise from doubt. Any exercise of ego-will is based on the doubt of what is true. From false confidence comes disobedience to what is right (obedience to temptation). Physical changes appear through the invisible fall. Observing those changes, we experience guilt. To ease the pain of conscience come the allies of the guilty nature—doubt and emotion—to rescue your pride.

The unseen, unholy spirit who controls the doubt-emotion-thought process speaks to you in your mind and offers you enticing morsels of resentment, the substance which your ego needs for its false sense of security. After all, if you puff up as a judge you can forget *you* are the criminal being judged. Can you see that there is a satanic suggestion as well as a hypnotic suggestion? Satanic suggestion poisons the soul, while hypnotic suggestion affects only the mind—the psychological process. But Satan can use your suggestibility to feed your need to doubt and to judge others, and thus further corrupt your soul.

The spirit outside you, inside others, gets inside and speaks to your soul with its power over your psychological processes.

This is the way all souls are convicted, swayed under the satanic rule. And this spirit of persuasion, which presently compels the world to follow the forbidden path, does so through its inherent power to make people doubt what is true. Through its power over your emotions, it keeps you upset all the time. You function according to its will on earth as it is in hell, whether you like it or not.

The underlying reason why the Satan principle works so well is our lack of faith (not knowing or not wanting to realize what is right). In politics, in medicine and in religion, the truth is suppressed in one way or another, even in democracy.

Our terrible need for someone to generate emotion in us is a kind of "love," even when that emotion is hate. And so it comes to pass that we cannot resist loving (clinging to) all sorts of evil because of its power to make us doubt what is true, ease our sense of guilt through keeping us preoccupied with loving or hating, and thus to restore pride and confidence in ourselves.

Even positive thinking can be another form of doubting

the truth, through its power to inspire confidence and faith in the wrong way.

Indeed, all who sin are slaves!

Can you see how incredibly subtle this process is? We are inherently and irresistibly programmed by the wrong spirit. This wicked spirit is more believable than God in that it comforts and seductively speaks to us through the intellect in which it has us all emotionally trapped. Lost in our minds, we think that our judgments are right and that what it wants is what we want. We are deceived into believing that our need for the trappings and tinsel of sin is an adventure in real life, while all we are doing is feeding our ego false happiness and innocence.

You can hardly help believing in whoever believes in you. Your tendency to be taken in by such people comes from the excitement you feel when their praise tempts you to doubt that anything is wrong with you. To become dependent on those who believe in you is to end up building your existence on dry bones in hell.

To truly resolve this highly sophisticated problem requires a deep realization: THERE IS NO NEED TO STRUGGLE WITH YOURSELF HERE, FOR ONCE YOU HAVE SENSE ENOUGH TO STOP SAVING YOURSELF, REVELATION ALONE HAS THE RESOLVING POWER TO SAVE YOU FROM THE HYPNOSIS OF SIN.

If you believe *into* what is right in your heart, if you now will hold fast with deep faith and conviction, new emotions will never arise. Old beliefs and emotions (upon which your false life has been built) will reappear and then dissolve.

There is a special passage in the Scripture which covers

174

everything that has been said here so far. In the King James Version we read:

> "My brethren, count it all joy when ye fall into divers temptations, knowing this, that the trying of your faith worketh patience. But let patience have her perfect work, that ye may be perfect and entire, lacking nothing."
> —James 1:2

Realize, the futility of struggle, and you will be saved from the guilt and the emotion of struggle, and from the disgrace of saving face. For willful struggle is evidence of a (faithless) sinner, aided by emotion, trying to save himself. But through emotion comes the sin of saving yourself from sin. That, too, is another attempt at restoring faith in yourself. For the very fact of not believing in what is greater than you challenges you to solve your own problems and thus casts into you the agony of struggling pridefully against God.

Any idea or answer that does not come down from above rises from your imagination. Remember that the fall to imagination constitutes the doubt which causes deep anxiety. Without strength that is based in deep knowing (faith) you are then left alone in your imagination to fight ideas with more ideas based on anger and fear. Emotion rises to give animal strength and comfort to the soul in its failing.

Whenever your ego is unable to locate that special contradictory idea to counter evil's power of suggestion, then it feels bound to suffer the agony of being converted (resentfully) to another's will.

Resentment is like candy in that it provides unhealthy nourishment, strength and security for the errant self.

175

Resentment toward another is the way you reject the truth about yourself. Puffing up in self-righteousness, you add guilt to guilt. So then you come full circle, and find yourself doubting your own judgment even more. The more *false* confidence you have, the more this leads to greater conflict about it, hence to a need to doubt the truth through more resentment.

Resentment is an emotion of judgment that strengthens your ego in its rejection of the truth so that you don't have to see that you are wrong. You are caught up in a judgment which momentarily provides you with a false sense of confidence and righteousness. And then, when resentment backfires into guilt, you often counter your guilt in the opposite way (that also leads to guilt) — that is, by getting approval. Either way, your life is based on the services of deception. You love the deceiver and you also love to judge him. He has got you coming and going!

No concept can save you except the realization that no concept can save you. You shall realize the truth, and the truth will make you free.

Sometimes you dwell in one compartment of your mind as a refuge from, and to forget, the turmoil in another part. You can also emotionally and traumatically change cultures and idea-sources to keep from seeing. One emotional experience can seem to save you from the grip of another.

You could, for example, rebel or escape from the guilt of having religion forced on you by "surrendering" traumatically to an opposite cause. The same holds true with marriage and other personal relationships. Going from the frying pan into the fire, your will is always involved with the agony of trying to save itself. In your

176

rebellion you think you want this religion, or that mate. You think freedom is doing the opposite of what others want of you—it isn't. The rebellion is wrong, and the reinforcement of that rebellion by another person or another cause is just another trap of hell.

As I have said before, doubting the true self we have left behind always has the effect of emotionally reinforcing the pride of being. We are naturally fascinated and excited by everyone who believes in us. Take a good hard look at how that principle applies to your own life. You will see an emotional child of pride growing, emotionally drawing to it ideas and people that help it more perfectly doubt God.

A red-blooded male can hardly resist the acceptance and invitation of a loose female. Why? Because her acceptance inspires his ego to doubt the truth of what he is and restores to him the idea that his malehood is manhood. The presence of evil can have this same comforting effect in your mind. You can sometimes feel something in you drawing you into some kind of velvety, dark security—that is the presence of evil making you doubt.

How can an ego determined to see itself as God be wrong about its choice? To lose faith in the wrong way it is going would wreck the whole system of pride.

Now, let's take another step closer to reality and look at this thing called choice and what it is that chooses. Choice is the prerogative of God. Decision-making, then, is part of the doubt/emotion/guilt syndrome. You are guilty of playing God, and "God," not wanting to be wrong, is forced to doubt truth in order to remain "God" by exercising choice.

There is a fascinating mystique in the process of goal

setting and in decision-making. It is not so much a matter of what is chosen; it is more the exercise of choice itself that is so fascinating and so compulsive. We are compelled to choose, even though we know those choices will lead to tragedy.

Judgment, you see, is an exercise of ego-will desperately striving to express its plan. A plan through which "God" makes himself known to his creatures requires knowledge and decisions. The need to make decisions draws ideas with which judgments are made and that, in turn, generates emotion. Caught up in dreams and scheming, you become emotionally alive (in that lower way) and, forgetting truth and guilt, you experience those illusory feelings of hope in your glorious destiny and greatness. That is the ecstasy which leads to the agony. However, by repeating the exercise of judgment again and again we can temporarily forget the agony (in ecstasies which lead to greater agonies).

Your ego can find a strange security in the decision-making process—that is, until you make so many mistakes that you are reminded of your fallibility. Then you develop so much guilt that you fear to make decisions, and you get caught up in deciding not to decide. Still, you are deciding, playing God and becoming more and more guilty.

The original sin lay in doubting the truth, and to this day there is an awful, mysterious ego-consolation in every secret doubt. To the degree that you lack faith, doubt causes emotion to rise. And such emotion, even when it appears in the form of fear, provides a short-lived sense of ego-security. The belief in the lie (which makes us doubt what is true) makes us fear the truth. Then it seems that the truth is from something bad, when it is really you who are bad in the Truth-Presence.

Now that you know what pressure does to people—it disables true belief—never be a pressure-source. Never pressure others to believe in you or what you say. Merely state facts in a timely way. And stand back from your own personal feelings if people pressure you. Never allow people to make you doubt yourself or make you fall prey to resentment. If you speak with faith and conviction, reckon on people trying to make you doubt yourself and what you see in them. They will want you to doubt yourself so that they can then believe in themselves. You will be hurt when you try to help. You will be rejected for your faith and accepted only for being a phony liar. Indeed, threatened parents often drive their innocent children mad by making them doubt themselves for the sake of the parents' own ego-security.

Rebellious people can be purposely irresponsible in order to set you up to be a familiar pressure-source so they can maintain a false righteousness based on their rebellion against you. Conformists are likewise unable to function without pressure to motivate them. Without pressure (which makes you the bad guy and liberates them from conscience), people are bared to themselves and that means realizing guilt. They need evil pressure because it upsets and helps them *doubt* that they are slaves of pressure. Therefore, don't pressure and you will help them to realize the truth whether they like it or not. (Incidentally, there is also a healthy, loving kind of pressure which comes from *what* is right rather than *who* is right.)

Your will, operating through impatience, has the effect

of temporarily relieving people of their own anxiety and guilt, making them feel very right indeed in their compulsive service to you, or in their rebellion against you. Impatience (the energy of pride) continues to evolve pride and delusions. As a result, you can feel very frustrated and guilty when things get worse for the people you are trying to help. Watch out for that impatient spirit operating in you, blocking out the light. Without will, there are no feelings of frustration and guilt, no feelings of responsibility for failing or, for that matter, succeeding.

The guilt you feel when your will backfires may very well make you emotionally capitulate to the person you are trying to save. It is not unusual to take on the characteristics of the drunk or drug addict you are trying to help, or even the criminal you are trying to reform. Why? Simply because *you* (without faith) would be taking your motivation from pressure and challenge, unconsciously *cultivating* the error in the victim to serve your energy need for judgment and self-righteousness through emotion. Through resenting the sinner for not reforming, you create for yourself the emotion you need to restore confidence and a false sense of righteousness. (There's that doubt again.)

Be apprised of this: people have a nose for what is going on inside your head. Your motive radiates. Emotionally charged fears, worries, scheming and planning can be picked up through a sort of osmosis of psychic induction. For this reason, Jesus taught us not to rehearse our conversations or defenses beforehand. Any preplanned arguments or defenses which arise in the mind are either implanted by manipulators or read by them through your emotions. Remember how pressure introduces thoughts through emotion. And all the emotions which are based in doubt feed the power of the wicked over you in your living hell.

Be careful, too, about bringing realizations down to an intellectual-remembrance level. Don't brag or talk about them to puff up your ego. Don't expose or openly discuss your secret plans, revelations and hopes, for other people will surely foil you and exploit you through your ambitions.

Error is conceived and born in secret. Therapeutically speaking, when a secret of error is exposed to the light, the problem is cured and its plan is disabled. But the same principle holds for truth. That is why you must not brag. Be quiet, unassuming and gentle, not given to prediction.

A voice (your ego-self) sometimes comes up from the depths of your unconsciousness to grab the glory of your realizations. You can get a tingle of excitement from saying deep things. Sometimes it will seem as though you are centered in your mouth. The mouth is directly connected to the intellectual process, which in turn is connected to the will operating through your emotions.

The mouth speaks on behalf of vanity. The mouth of the ego is the prideful counterpart to the word of God. By words, we try to effect changes in the lives of others. We get high if we succeed, and threatened, angry and frustrated when we fail. Either way, we are in trouble. Do you see how all this can have something to do with proving yourself?

Therefore, although truth can be heard and recognized, it may not effectively change the sinner who hears it. Through emotion, he may seize upon the memory form of truth and use it to puff up like a proud peacock. Again, behold the principles of false faith and doubt.

Meaningful change comes only through *understanding*. On the other hand, every choice you make that is based upon the *knowledge* you acquire (even sound philosophical truths) has to do with your trying to prove that special something to yourself (that you are God, that you are right) through the very exercise of choice.

You scan the horizon for knowledge. You weigh each decision. You are careful to do things exactly right, never wrong. Yet no matter how "right" you do it, you never *feel* right even if you *act* right. There is that lingering uncertainty, blossoming into guilt feelings which lure you back again and again to the ego-exercise, the ecstasy and agony of doubt that reinforces faith in your Godsmanship amid the mad babble of your mind.

Growing insecurity (you think you are God but you discover you are not) drives you into the delirium of decision-making even when *you know* those decisions are going to turn out wrong. You see, sin can be forgotten in the act of making decisions, and that is the ecstasy. Remember what I said about making decisions being the ecstasy of an evolving God. Discovering the futility of it all is the agony.

Then comes the moment when you begin to fear the consequences of your own decision-making, because the observed folly which results from it forces you to doubt your righteousness. To avoid that, you may hand over the responsibility to others. If they are right, you take the credit for choosing them, showing your good judgment of people. And if they are wrong, you feel superior by judging their mistakes. You elect the kinds of failures who love to run other people's lives, who never have to suffer the consequences of those decisions. (You do.)

Government bureaucrats fall into this last category. The more you suffer from their mistakes, the more power you must give them to solve problems by decisions (painless to them) which cause bigger problems that keep on multiplying. So it comes to pass that they can enjoy the pleasure of making decisions without directly experiencing the repercussions which prove their folly. I tell you, the whole world is stark, raving mad. Don't doubt it, and don't resent it when you see it.

Government running and ruining our lives is one reason for the people being driven into a psychotic state. In any psychotic state the victim's pathetic need to make judgments (because of guilt) soon becomes narrowed down to petty things, such as whether he should turn right or left, stand up or sit down.

As long as you live in a mortal body, you are more or less vulnerable to both subliminal and obvious suggestions. The only thing that can save you is to realize it when it is happening. Scan your thoughts and feelings continuously, and you will live unto God.

You cannot de-program yourself or others, because any de-programming is merely re-programming. The only meaningful form of counter suggestion comes from faith in the light in one's own private experience. Realization is that other, deep way of knowing and deciding. And faith produces the divine emotion of strength called love. The root of this new life is not in this world—you will live in the world, but you will not be of it.

Remember, the root of your ego-problem is that subtle need to doubt truth, to be God and to be liberated from the anxiety of the masquerade. The motivator has a need to be needed. He (or she) is dependent on your weakness. His vile job is to fulfill that need and keep you happy and weak. While you believe that all is well, hell continues to live through you.

Those who presently control you fear your awakening. They are desperate. By hook or by crook, they must make you doubt yourself. Beware, then—just as you begin to seek and see things clearly, just as you are about to repent of what you are, they can try to rob you of your precious repentance by believing in you, and perhaps by bestowing upon you all the sympathy and success you ever wanted. *Careful—watch that resentment toward them.*

It is easy to resent people who want to rob you of the exquisite purging pain of repentance. Be careful. Don't fall into that old trap. Their motive should be more clear to you now. Also, watch those who try to sell you a religion that says God loves you *as you are.* The god who accepts you as you are is robbing you of repentance and change. That god is always Satan, even when he is dressed up as a Christian minister of the gospel.

Those hypocrites seem so considerate, so understanding and loving, so nice. What could be wrong with that? How can one complain? You can't—you are blocked by the supportive "goodness" of their god. Such grace-robbers are offering you nothing more than salvation from salvation. It is another form of doubting the true God and restoring faith in pride, yourself and Satan.

Until you learn the mystery of faith, of resolving your need for people and for the resentment, fear, emotional love and pleasure that they provide, you will never be free from the grip of the Satan principle.

10 Democracy, Hypocrisy & Revolution

Beware of the "one God, one vote" rhetoric of the serpent. A true democracy is where the majority wills or "votes" for the one God's rule on this earth. Remember the words of William Penn: "If men do not find God, they will be ruled by tyrants."

Sensible women seek the dominance of a wise husband. The rest appoint a weak male whom they can dominate and manipulate. In essence, the former relationship is a healthy democracy. After all, a woman doesn't *have* to marry. The latter represents the kind of democracy we have now, where the sinful masses elect idol-politicians who justify them in their sins. In Sodom and Gomorrah, too, everyone had his own lifestyle, and each did what was good in his own eyes—and as a reward for their foolishness, God destroyed them.

So the problem with a democracy is the people. With good people comes a sound, workable democracy. Otherwise, you have a democracy in name only and that begins the nightmare and tyranny of "hypocrisy," leading to revolution and dictatorship.

Another danger to democracy is the misuse of duly

authorized power. Authority must be just. A husband must be considerate of his wife's real needs as a human being, as well as firm with any foolishness. If he uses his God-given manly role to oppress and use his wife, then it is a dictatorship, not a marriage. And if the husband is weak, you have a female dictatorship in the name of marriage which leads to the usual rebellion, treason and coups against the tyrant.

It is not the institution of marriage that is the problem, just as the problem does not lie with democracy or religion per se. Those institutions are basically wholesome and noble, and they are God's gift to His people. But when they are misused and misunderstood, you have democracy, marriage and Christianity in name only. They become a system of justice which unjust people hide behind in order to exploit others legally.

That eventually makes many believe that democracy doesn't work, marriage doesn't work, religion doesn't work and free enterprise doesn't work, and there arises a feeling of wanting to tear it all down. But then what would you have left? Dictatorship without hypocrisy! Soon after that we would find ourselves in revolt again, setting up another democracy as the man sets up the other woman to support his revolution against his wife. Sometimes he gets another dictator, and sometimes *he* is the dictator.

Without perfect integrity, marriage cannot fulfill its proper destiny, and neither can government.

A woman is wise who picks a wise man to rule her. It is the guilt, the sin and the serpent in the woman which fears a man's dominating wisdom, and which consciously or unconsciously wishes to project and cultivate its own kind on earth so that it can rule amid the resulting confusion. So when the weakness of men and the wickedness of women cohabit, they produce hypocrisy or dictatorship and never-ending turmoil and suffering.

Remember what I said at the beginning of this book: culture always rises as civilization falls. The madness of culture can be expressed in countless ways, and one of the most dangerous is when it masquerades as civilized democracy, for that tempts the people to rebel against what is most beneficial to them, exposing them, without the protection of God's law, to the dangers of vicious dictatorship.

If it is to survive, democracy must learn to distinguish between social psychopaths and genuine leaders. Unfortunately, because of an inherent prejudice in our human nature, we are more responsive to psychopaths because they are more believable than the honest men they mimic. Unless the people learn to distinguish between them, we can look forward to nothing but spiraling misery and suffering, leading to an ultimate holocaust from which few will survive.

The social psychopath actually hates the democracy that he pretends to love. Social psychopaths are the world's most dangerous villains. We are mainly concerned here with the social psychopath because, in the ordinary course of events, few of us run in the same track as the criminal psychopath.

From the day he is born, the social psychopath's soul embraces evil and hates good, and he exists for one reason only—to destroy. Destruction is his creation. If there is some dangerous atomic project, the psychopathic scientist will recommend it; if it is valuable to society, he will be against it. If he can help you, he will hurt you instead, and you will pay dearly somewhere down the line for whatever favors he does extend.

The social psychopath can destroy you with his love just as easily as with his more obvious wickedness. That evil becomes very apparent in those moments of horror when you find yourself trapped by the very trust he seduced you to give him.

"But," you may ask, "if a man be so evil through and through, how can he appear to be so good? How does he acquire the seemingly virtuous traits of character that lure you into believing him?"

The first stage of a two-part answer is this: by his sheer hatred of good does the psychopath acquire the external attributes of a sincere person. Indeed, it is commonplace to acquire the surface virtues of those you envy. For instance, I knew a man who was unconsciously compelled to hate great musicians so as to acquire their talents. Needless to say, it was through his hatred of his mother's ambition for him that he evolved her ambition as his own. And so his mother's will operating in him went on to envy others greater than himself so as to evolve itself more completely in him. Through envy and jealousy, the lost soul evolves an imitation of the goodness he covets in others. By putting other people on, he gets the "righteousness" from them which he cannot obtain from God.

Of all people, the social psychopath is in the least "danger" of truly becoming the good he hates, because *genuine* goodness can never evolve through one's hatred of it. If goodness appears in that way, it is merely in the superficial, hypocritical form.

Now let us talk about the second phase of the answer as to why psychopathic hypocrisy is difficult to discern.

188

This has to do with your guilt, a prejudice of ego that makes a phony, psychopathic personality more acceptable to you than the *principle* he is supposed to represent. Personal involvement with a personality helps you escape reality (principle) and evolve, as it were, your own sense of worth. Here, the psychopath is the model who prostitutes himself for this purpose and for power.

Psychotics, escaping from their guilt (induced by other psychopaths in their past), are drawn to hero-worship great personalities,† trying to willfully acquire through evolution those virtues lost through corruption and denied them through pride.

So-called Christians are really psychotics who try to take on Christ's goodness by the osmosis of such temptation as I have described. Among religious cultists one can find the most lowly serpents sweet-talking flocks of glory-seeking psychotics who also hate the truth. You don't have to be a psychopath to hate truth—you can be a psychotic who employs the services of a phony religious personality who allows you to use him for that purpose. And there you have the whole rotten world in a nutshell.

Without exception, Jesus freaks have the utmost contempt for Jesus and His God. The guilt of their vile, egocentric lives (many of them have a history of drugs, violence and crime) drives them to take refuge in and to imitate the very truth they once ran from and still despise. They take refuge in Christian religiosity not only to escape persecution by the indwelling Truth, but also to seem to join that which they secretly hate when there is nowhere else to run. People hate God because they want

†From the Latin *persona*, meaning "mask."

to *be* the God they hate. *And they also wish to discredit true Christianity by their masquerade.* When defeated, all weasels will join their enemies, but they do so in order to conquer from within.

The effect of the Jesus freaks' zeal, ranting and raving is:

1) to drive decent people away from the very religion that could save them, and

2) to attract their own kind to the bloodsucking advantages of "respectability" and the terrible, confusing power of such false goodness.

The Jesus-freak psychotic can accept a psychopathic cult leader mainly because that kind of phony goodness does not threaten his equally phony need for a religious cover and a "righteous" identity. Religious psychopaths specialize in building slave empires through reinforcing the psychotics' delusions of grandeur. These evil shepherds (social psychopaths) zealously guard their flocks from the horrors of reality, and together, they all try to save the innocents (who seem like sinners to them).

Many careless experiences with psychopaths lead to sin, and sin leads to decadence, fear and guilt. Often the indwelling, alien pride of the ordinary sinner does not permit him to repent so as to receive grace directly from God. So what does he do? He willfully sets up a personality on a pedestal and empowers that psychopath to tempt him to believe in himself again. What temptation takes, it also seems to have the power to give back.

Remember, between the tempter and the tempted there is always that exchange going on, so that one can acquire an apparent goodness by responding, just as one can acquire an evil nature by responding. Alas, that experience

190

with apparent goodness only reinforces the indwelling sin. Eventually, that can drive a person to commit suicide or murder in the name of good. The Crusades and the Holocaust were notable examples of this kind of barbaric human sacrifice—absolute wickedness carried out in the name of righteousness.

A sure sign of a psychotic is that he will work for a cause no matter how just or unjust it is without ever questioning his leader.

Joiners are psychotics to the end, like the crew of Captain Ahab going after the white whale in *Moby Dick*. Or they are quietly evolving the identity of the leadership by unquestioned obedience. Joiners are deadly; they are traitors against conscience. And these scoundrels find their last refuge in religion just as often as in patriotism.

When religion is used for escape, the leader's agreement with evil evolves as violence in the followers. Those who fight religious and patriotic wars are created and sanctioned by the subtle hell of their sanctimonious leaders. Certain Anglo-Saxon, so-called Christian patriots are actually products of *Churchianity*.

All who seek to belong must sacrifice themselves for the sake of a new identity. That is not too hard to do, because the victim's ego doesn't have to change; besides, he thinks he is getting a better identity (when he is actually getting one much worse).

By the classic syndrome of clinging to what corrupted them and by their mindless obedience for the sake of approval, psychotic joiners can usually manage to stay ahead of guilt. This displacement of identity through seduction manifests as an insatiable appetite for destruction. Just as their innocence was destroyed, sacrificed for the glory of their cause (by their leader), so must they find their own sacrificial lambs. Innocent people now must be sacrificed to appease their guilt. What we have here is the basis of violent racism.

In your personal relationships, the bottom line is this: don't join or belong to anything.

Also beware of nice, easygoing friends who do lots of favors and who cannot or will not say no to you, who act proper (in front of you) just to get your approval. Such as these are weasels who want to make you into an authority which you should never be.

Such as these are psychotics who want to create their very own psychopath to love them and to cloak them with a righteous identity. They need false goodness to make up for true goodness which their secret rottenness prevents them from obtaining through God's grace. And if you fail to detect what is going on, they will eventually destroy you. Elvis was a typical victim of this kind of role-playing who became too rich and too guilty to stop playing the game.

Let such people have the cutting edge of truth. Be quick to notice indiscretion, and don't let things go too long. If there is good in them, they will appreciate the pain your honesty may incur; otherwise, they will drop you like a hot potato and find themselves another cause to get caught up in. Also, watch out for people who cry and carry on when you correct them. Here again, it could be the sin of the psychotic at work displaying sorrow and anguish before you. They want to raise you up to the stature of God in order to get "God's" approval.

You may be tempted to excuse such wickedness, but since you are *not* God, being sympathetic and sorry for people only releases them from guilt and gives them license to be wrong again. Your part in this can make you feel guilty too, but they can train you to relieve your guilt by "forgiving" theirs.

Most quiet people are seething volcanoes inside, never openly speaking their secret mind about you because they want to get your approval. In no way do they want you to be honest with them either, and to this end they will curry your favor, bow down and let you do whatever you want.

But only evil will service their kind of wicked need. They submit and obey so meekly, never saying no and never criticizing you to your face, because they want to preserve your wicked love to sustain their own secret wicked self. They want your pretense, phony righteousness, happiness and smiles to become theirs also.

You almost can't help liking people like that because, without realizing what has happened, you have already become alike, and a little bit of yourself is in them. Look at women who admire homosexual men and you will see that principle at work—they love the projection of their nature, as God loves His own creation.

Even if you are not really a psychopath through and through, you will, nevertheless, feel Satan being drawn up in you if you serve these fiends. And if you are a man, you will come to know what it is like to be tormented as women are for role-playing. (Men put women on pedestals to get their support.)

The social psychopath begins life with a total contempt for God and for good people. But hating good people, he can begin to look like them and speak like them. As a student, he may be attracted to principled models. Acting

193

the role of a psychotic, he submits to authority for the sake of becoming that authority; he is a good pupil and learns quickly by interreacting with the "victim-mentor." Sadly, the nice people he associates with are often adversely affected, because he tempts them in order to take away their virtue, leaving something of his wicked-self behind. Believe it or not, he can even take away your youth, life, health and creative intelligence.

For many years he may not overtly betray anyone. Like the good spy that he is, he bides his time until he is "good" and ready to serve his master, Satan. If you are observant, you can detect him monitoring you for ideas and weaknesses continuously. His creativeness is limited to picking the brains of the more intelligent around him, and he survives by fooling them and putting them on, stealing their ideas and imitating their motivation.

As I said before, it is easier for most people to respect a social psychopath than an honest-to-goodness honest person. The reason should be much clearer by now: honesty threatens the psychotic ego. Each one of us has an ego which, until the age of enlightenment, feels intimidated by reality and tries to escape the pain of that through being drawn to comforting personalities.

Hypocrisy rarely disturbs the psychotic ego. On the contrary, the apparent good in the psychopath is quick to praise your "worth," and *you tend to respond with the same feelings he or she expresses about you.* But do you know what happens? Although you seem to improve in his presence, in reality you get worse. As you pick up the surface behavior, you also take on the more secret evil and its purpose. In turn, the conflict you feel inside makes the psychopath seem more attractive and compels you to look up to him even more—to the end that he will glorify you again.

Perhaps you do accomplish great things together—with you doing all the work (to hang on to his approval of the identity he has sown in you) and him getting all the credit, money and power. But you may not mind this a bit because the greater he becomes, the greater you can seem to be becoming. The greater you make him, the more glorious your reflection of him (which you think of as your own, original personality) seems to be. But in reality you are becoming sick, poor and wretched. Desperately caught up in images, the illusion of your perfection becomes more and more complete and you cannot put your finger on what is going wrong with your life and family affairs. How can you!

Perhaps you will experience the classic moment of awakening where you see the hideous evil behind the smiling, psychopathic mask. But here is where your hatred of the deception evolves yet another phase of evil's projection. Through your seething resentment, evil insinuates itself into your life more and more completely, and soon you find yourself crying out for its supportive wickedness as well as its supportive phony love to mask the greater wrong growing up inside you.

Social psychopaths have never at any time been servants of the people. You have been their slave all along, a slave of the illusion of goodness they served to your ego through the power you gave them to excite you and distract you from a guilty conscience. Unwillingness to face the reality of even this fact compels you to place that evil back on the pedestal to serve you.

The social psychopath is a leader whom most of the

people love until they see him for what he is. And then, just maybe, they will hate him—but at that time his spirit will be cast into those who destroy him. Evil never dies—it evolves or projects its hell from person to person, and as each one dies to evil he gives the devil life in human form.

Those who do see the psychopath's hidden nature see it mostly because they have experienced firsthand betrayal. At first, they may try to sound the alarm for those who are still fascinated under the psychopath's spell. But it is useless. Each of you has to feel the terrible pain of the psychopath's treachery and confusion personally, and even then you may be too afraid, too guilty to awaken. The reason why is that without a psychopath's presence to cling to, your own guilt is bared (but you think that guilt comes from the thought of betraying him).

Life's experiences are like many doors. Each door seems to offer happiness, advantages and adventure. It seems so right as you enter, but then the door closes behind you and you are trapped. You are afraid to go back, so on you go to the next door and the next; and the last doorway is death, with hell beyond.

What I am trying to say is that most (not all) leader-types are social psychopaths who bleed and exploit the masses from behind a personality mask of respectability. And the great majority revel in that phoniness. Through science, politics, religion, education and medicine, psychopaths have appeared to give you solutions to the problem of sin, to restore your lost dignity, but all the while they are really eating you alive. They are the ushers at those doors.

Lurking in all republics and democracies are treacherous forces which exist to demoralize the citizens into

196

tearing down the system. But when they do, those forces are still there, unmasked.

In every war against injustice, the better cause eventually wins out, but then, strangely, it evolves the next tyrannical system that must be brought down.

Soldiers come home with the identity of the enemy they fought alive and well in them. Without realizing it, they have brought it home to infect their families, friends and coworkers.

The enemy, you see, is not a person. It is a *spirit*. For instance, a wicked man can tempt you to kill him (and perhaps give you good cause to). But if you do so out of anger, you find to your horror that you have become infected with the very evil that you thought you had destroyed. There it is, alive and well, mocking from its new home in you—and now you are the new tyrant.

The same principle holds true in society. Castro, who came in as a liberator, himself became a dictator as bad as the tyrant he had vanquished. When the Russian Orthodox Church became the instrument of the wickedness it despised in doctrine, Communism brought the Church down. Look at what has become of Communism now!

Here in America and in England also, we find conditions similar to those that prevailed in pre-war Germany before Hitler took power, while Germany and perhaps Japan now enjoy our former position. A more detailed look at this puzzle will follow.

There are many variations of this principle of becoming like the evil you hate—or admire. You can begin to admire the enemy you once hated, because so much of him (or her) got inside you.

Governments and the media fail to realize what they do

by upsetting and gingering us up against an enemy like Naziism or the North Vietnamese. Our reactions tend to make us over in the image of the hated enemy *and soon we see atrocities in our own homes.* I am very sure the Communists are using this principle to destroy us. Threats, intrigues and atrocities, eagerly reported by sensation-seeking media, make us fighting mad. By this means, our enemies are able to use our own system to plant the seeds of Communism (or any *ism*) in the American mind. Believe it or not, many enemy sympathizers have already been created in precisely this fashion.

Hatred *always* divides the populace into evil groups which evolve one another: those which rebel against and those which conform to the object of hate. Be careful about my meaning here. *I am not implying that we should be passive* in the sense that we say, "Ho hum," hoping that wickedness will go away. What I *am* saying is that we must learn how to deal strongly with phoniness and wickedness, with a special non-violent force *that is not born of hate.* Hate is the reaction of obedience to evil which puts the tempter's purpose within you. If this be truth, you cannot afford to allow yourself to luxuriate in that emotion. You must find the opposite kind of obedience (obedience to what is right) which will draw to you patience and love with which to meet stress.

It is through resentment that you become like the mother you hate, whether you can see it or not. As a male, you can get so close to your mother that you become a homosexual. As a female, you can become the impatient, man-teasing bitch your mother used to be. Or you might police yourself to avoid being as pushy and manly as your mother. In rebellion against the spirit of the mannish, dominating tyrant-momma, you play the submissive feminine role to a weak male, hoping that by helping him to feel like more of a man you will assume the identity of a woman. But what happens? That form of submission becomes tantamount to conquest. You discover to your horror that this was precisely how your mother got your father! This same principle operates in democracies, with the government playing the seductive, momma/female role.

Running away from his dominating mother and his weak (or rebellious, violent) father, a man seeks the support of a slinky female who surrenders (apparently conceeding to his authority). Every corrupted person is drawn to wickedness like a fly to dung; he must have what violated him to love and to hate.

What you see in marriage is what invariably occurs in free elections where the people are supposed to elect their "loving" leaders. Remember again the Satan principle: who made you what you are, loves you just *as* you are. You marry a woman who supports you against the dominance of your mother (or a former wife), and she turns out to be another tyrant! You stop smoking only to start overeating, and you are a slave either way.

The masses, with few individual exceptions, are under an unconscious compulsion to elect (marry) a government that serves their egos. Alas, by serving, a seductive government mothers the people and gains ascendency over their minds and lives. Coming to the rescue of the people it cripples, government weakens them even more, so that they have an ever greater need for the services of the momma-politicians (for which they pay through the nose). The growing demands of a "loving" government on the people's paycheck is like a demanding wife with her husband, and it has the same effect on the nation. Some "husbands" rebel; others drive themselves harder to please their god, who is never satisfied; others defect and change sides.

In a situation like this, it is not long before loyal workers start having nervous breakdowns, and in one way or another they rebel against the burden of taxation to pay for the welfare of the criminals and dropouts. Incentive leaves them. Productivity sags. With a diminishing tax base, the government is forced to print money to keep up the "benefits" and to buy votes, desperately trying to hold its power. And you know the rest of the story...

Again, I want to make it clear that the enemy is never a person or a government—it is the spirit of evil. And no matter what form of tyranny you live under, you tend to become infected by the spirit behind it. Let me refer again to the beginning of this book, where I stated that culture rises as true civilization falls. Civilizations have administrations, but cultures have governments which try to take the place of God in people's lives.

If you fight the enemy and lose, you remain a psychotic victim. If you fight and win, you become like what you hated. Hatred makes one person serve and another rebel. And so it comes to pass that evil turns brother against brother, husband against wife. It sets people up against good forms of government as well as bad ones.

Only the supportive evil in others will rise to placate the implanted evil in you. And their evil will eventually exploit you. The stage is then set for rebellion against the iron will of the tyrant or for total submission, as in a cult. Rebellion often takes the form of irresponsible behavior,

200

drunkenness, drug addiction or crime. It could even lead to revolution itself, with the revolutionaries drawing out of the pit a greater evil to support them in their cause.

The indwelling evil is supported in rebellion by our seductive "friends," and when such as these become our leaders, betrayal is sure to be the order of the day. There is betrayal in marriage and there is also betrayal in government. The husband betrays the wife who spoils him rotten, and the wife betrays her husband by revealing herself to be a tyrant instead of a lover; a similar relationship exists between the people and their government. And if we try to get free, we always find the same enemy in a new and disguised form. The sinner's liberty is not freedom—he is just freed from the frying pan so that he can jump into the fire.

Marriage is not the problem. Democracy is not the problem. It is the spirit of evil which is the problem. The guile in us all solicits support from the friendly evil in others, and we find this comforting, but debilitating, process going on in all of our relationships—marriage, friendship and government. Wickedness supporting weakness is the invisible rule operating in all dictatorships, and that same quality is there in those effeminate leaders who rise to the occasion of our prideful need in a democracy.

Soon after we have built a model system of law and order with blood, sweat and tears, the selfish, deceitful spirit of leadership begins to make itself felt, and things start going wrong all over again.

Exploited by business and taxes, people begin to rebel against pushy, unreasonable, "wifey" governments. Rebels pride themselves in their rebellion because hating wrong helps them think they are right (they are not). Conformists pride themselves in their psychotic patriotic behavior because it is rewarded by the system that created it. But it is the nature of governments to become ever more oppressive, never satisfied with the power they have. So the rebel ranks begin to swell. Even squares start breaking laws and cheating the system in order to survive. Eventually, they will be so immoral or so mad that they will tear down the government, as if democracy itself, with its marvelous system of laws, were the problem. As I pointed out, it is the spirit *behind* law and order which wants to make slaves out of everyone that is the problem.

Again, marriage provides a good parallel: without realizing the power they have and what they are doing to their husbands, wives make their men into weaklings or beasts. Some wives feel troubled by their power, and yet don't know how to give it up; others revel in that power and feel threatened by the possibility of their husbands waking up. Some husbands don't know and don't want to know better. Others struggle to hold on to what is left of their self-respect by rebelling. Rebellion can take the form of breaking the marriage bonds and running with other women (flirting and sympathizing with other goverments) or just plain crime and revolution.

The hypocrisy of democracy, while pretending to promote and preserve decency, actually fosters social breakdown and revolution. Led by resentment, we consort with the enemy to get even and get free.

The guilt of hating may cause people to have sympathy for what they hate—and all the more so if what they hate is wicked, because capitulating to it can seem to be more honest, more in agreement with what they are really like inside.

You can become like the thing you hate in order to escape from your guilt. The hidden logic is this: when you feel guilty for hating, then it seems that if you sympathize, side or identify with the people you hated, you might be able to share the innocence you think *they* have (because you have the guilt). Add the subtlety of hating wrong to feel right, and before you know what is happening, you are no longer the law-abiding person you prided yourself in being; you become as vile and as violent as what you hate, and you become a rebel. In this manner, police officers often become lawless themselves, taking on the nature of the criminals they hunt down.

Believe it or not, subversives are actually the projection of a hypocritical society. The evil of an unjust judge, teacher, doctor or sick policeman creates hardened criminals. The more they try to cure the social problems for which they are secretly responsible, the worse their victims become, and the more the victims cling to the criminal psychopaths of an antisocial order for comfort.

Now the answer lies in awakening the people (husband) as well as the government (wife) of the people. If that is not done, democracy is in danger of losing its "husband" to another "woman." The other woman can be crime, Communism (or any other "ism"), decadence or outright revolution.

The entire system of social psychopaths and psychotic slaves is *immorally* legal. Rebels abandon law and order altogether, seeking freedom from its legal thievery, its straightjacket of debilitating, creeping tyranny. But one way or another, both conformists and rebels are lost to decadence, their characters deteriorate and evil slips into their souls. Think of it: religious hypocrites and social squares actually carry within them the seeds of their own destruction.

People begin to rebel against their jobs, as if there were something wrong with work itself. More and more time is spent now in drinking and smoking to drive away guilt, or in having nervous fits, destructive tantrums or total breakdowns. Then, within the framework of a legally free society, subtle, hidden forms of tyranny arise to meet the deterioration of the needy people—for instance, medicine, drugs and psychiatry. In every home, school, penal institution, factory and hospital, unparalleled tyranny exists, untouchable and legally protected.

Again, it is not the work or the system that is the problem. The problem is the enslaving momma-spirit, the driving force behind the work and the system that makes you feel as if you are a slave in hell.

As conflict grinds things to a halt, lieutenants of the respective systems of rebellion and conformity are compelled to find newer methods to motivate their "donkeys," until the "donkeys" begin to feel the futility that real donkeys can't feel. Some change sides (changing from dope addicts to false Christians, or vice versa, for example). But very few suffer a real change of heart.

If you ran from your oppressive, Bible-thumping parents (and didn't become a thumper yourself), you will be too lenient with your own children, and there is the evil again, expressing itself at the opposite end of the spectrum. You become a hypocritical parent with hypocritical friends to support your self-deception. And that is how your indwelling evil is reinforced and projected to your own rebellious or conforming offspring. Children can see in you what you can't (won't) see in yourself, and in hating you, they become on the outside what you are like on the inside. Evil is at work everywhere, setting mother against son, husband against wife and brother against brother.

If a black man offends you, you tend to think all black men are bad. Because of your reaction, you lose awareness with which to identify and deal effectively with the *spirit* of that person. Rebels see the system as the problem rather than the spirit that has made the system its tool, and so the evil operating in the system and in corrupt politicians can trick the evil in the rebels to tear down that system (and then get them for disobeying the law). Unfortunately, if that system which is torn down is democratic, what you have left is a nightmare of horror that we must fight if order is to be restored. And so the struggle begins again.

When will we understand that rebels are no different than the evil they hate? Rebellion is the tangible manifestation of its forerunner, the evil of hypocrisy, which is the matrix through which is projected real hell on earth.

11 The Power of Deception

Does it not seem strange that in spite of 8,000 years of history we never seem able to pinpoint the *cause* of human suffering? Yet it is staring us straight in the face every day of our lives, and we cannot see it. The reason we cannot is that *there is an inherent ego-weakness in all of us that allows us to be confused by what we see, and, furthermore, the same in us can confuse others.*

Everywhere you look, people are confusing one another and generally driving each other mad. Parents do it to children; governments do it to the people. Business, religion and medicine all do it, each in its own unique style. Your friends make you doubt yourself, and so do your enemies. What is more, you—yes, *you*—do it to others. And you probably do not see it when it is happening because you find pleasure in getting away with it. What a proud peacock you are after you have impressed someone with your knowledge or knocked him down to build yourself up.

In order to become a psycho-power, you must confuse; you must cause people to leave behind their own sensibilities so that they will rely on you as their savior.

And after you have destroyed their confidence and transferred their faith to you, you will hold the reins of power, life and security—such as it is. Your victims can only believe in themselves if you believe in them, and for the sake of your support, they will do anything. They will follow you to hell and back for your reassurance.

The entire world system is built upon a lie-base. The evil principality behind the scenes can only exist as long as it remains believable, as long as it is not seen for what it is. To become acceptable to people, you have to come down to their level; you simply cannot be yourself if you want to be accepted by the world. And when you are loved for not being yourself, you become less and less yourself; here you discover that you have been had. Here comes the guilt, attended by the need to be loved by what you will come to hate, and here, also, comes death.

The soul is a creature of belief. It cannot function without a reciprocal belief-relationship with something, even if that something is evil. If for any reason you fall to evil's persuasion, the guilt of that experience will always draw you back to the evil to "save" you from seeing what it has made of you. Thus, guilt makes it easier to believe in deception.

The wickedness of the psychopath and the conflict of the psychotic compel them to try to make you doubt what you see in them. Guilty people will drive you mad (to restore their false confidence) rather than face up to their wrongs. Nothing is sacred to them. They twist and distort everything to *upset* you into feeling inferior to their authority. They will even sacrifice the sanity and health of their own children.

The horror, madness and confusion everywhere originate through the power which big, dominant sinners have to confound and rule little sinners. Parents are especially guilty of this.

People who are guilty of past indiscretions tempt and sin automatically and compulsively. And this impatience in an authority figure confuses children, forcing them to doubt what they see. The parental sense of security depends upon right appearing to be wrong, and wrong appearing to be right. Sick parents "correct" children most when nothing is amiss. Nothing is said when their children really need correcting love—if they are not destroyed by impatience, they are rewarded, excused and praised for being ambitious, angry and greedy. One trick is to withhold what is naturally due a child and then give way to his resultant anger. That teaches the child to be wrong (angry) and it teaches him that he can have his way through rage and meanness.

You may even marry a person who has been more immoral and thus guiltier than you in order to feel right about yourself by comparison. Should you then find that he or she has some sense of value left, you might proceed to destroy that so that you can go on feeling comfortable about what you are, having what you want to have and doing what you crave. Men who marry older women often do so because they want a momma-wife who holds her power by excusing all indiscretion and taking her whimpering dog back no matter what.

The security, the power and the glory of evil rest in excusing the wrongs of the insane culture and in making normal people doubt what they see. The devil (incarnated in people) has authority over us *only so long as we are willful or can be made to doubt our own reason.*

Doubt is a reverse faith. The name of the game is *confusion*. Experts everywhere, in politics, the arts, religion and exact sciences, maintain their power through hidden ways of inducing very subtle forms of doubt in the masses and through offering them new ways of restoring their lost health and happiness through science and technology.

Unfortunately, a great majority of psychotics find pleasure in being degraded and made to doubt themselves. Remember the classic reason: to the great unwashed masses, *doubting the truth has the electric, revitalizing power to restore confidence in the ways of pride and sin.* For instance, the love of a woman gives pleasure to a man by making him doubt the truth about himself; being made to doubt that liberates his ego from guilt (and conscience) through the excitement of emotion.

Doubting truth was the original sin. The doubt which first separated man from God still causes insecurity and draws a man to seek reassurance about himself and his condition. Science claims that man came from apes, and woman accepts the ape as man. Any hint or reassurance that wrong is right or that ape is man drives the fallen man wild with delight, and it makes little difference whether that reassurance comes through love-shock or through hate-shock.

Worry is another (comforting) form of doubt. One can feel noble being worried for others. Worry is an emotional escape. Through worry we seek control of things and escape from the realization of our helplessness.

Positive thinking is yet another form of doubting truth. Here again, you (emotionally) think you are wonderful when your conscience is trying to show you otherwise. Positive thinking, being a direct support to the fallen ego, produces emotion needed to complete a false feeling of well-being.

It was belief in a lie that caused sin. The extension of that principle is that when we doubt that we are wrong, it is tantamount to another lie which sustains us in sin.

Beware of those people who take a liking to you without knowing what you are really worth. Your guilty nature finds it hard to resist the temptation to lose itself in that kind of adoration. As a sinner, you crave recognition to lift you out of the awareness of your depression and inferiority. A sensible person never finds pleasure in being praised (into doubting the truth about himself) the way willful, wicked people do. The trouble is that you may become resentful toward those who put you on and believe in you because that sets up conflict. But so does the resentment you feel toward them. So praise can be a pressure designed to get you both coming and going.

The comfort which kills is based on a lie. There are two kinds of security: one (real security) when you are right, and the other (false security) when you are wrong. The sinner *feels* alive (in the lower, animal way) and right when he is supported in his wrong, and that is the root of slavery and addiction.

Allow me to reexamine some concepts for the sake of clarity. Wherever culture has displaced civilization, evil, seductive people are embraced and placed high upon a pedestal for their ability to generate emotion and identity in the degenerating, dying masses. The arts, religion and politics become corrupted, and the lowest scum of the earth float entertainingly to the top.

Feelings appear as the ego is tempted and falls. That is to say, we feel most alive and righteous at the very moment we are becoming dead (and) wrong. Through the exciting trauma of temptation, evil enters into and parasites upon the soul. Temptation is attractive because it appears to give the ego eternal life as we obey it, but it is only a life that leads to death, one in which we serve the evil, motivating power.

The trauma of suffering is just as vital to the ego life as pleasure is. We develop a need for trauma to complete the infernal ego-life apart from God as a god ourself.

Remember that in culture everything is in reverse, compared with civilization. In a culture, the people become degenerating animals, clinging to and modeling themselves after their corrupter's image—it is all they have. Haven't you noticed how people go wild with delight over a nitwit performer making an ass out of himself by screaming, hollering, ranting, raving and shaking his body obscenely? It should be noted that these performers have talent only in that they know how to impart a sense of identity to the audience, making the "undead" feel gloriously alive through trauma. Psychotic people are happiest in the moment of corruption. The survival of their ego *demands* corruption and emotional excitement, pleasant or unpleasant.

Conversely, in order to survive as a real human being, you must find the *neutral zone of awareness* where there is no past, no future and no love/hate feelings. For where there is no selfish, animal feeling, there is the true experience of fulfillment and growth and, through it all, God's love for others. This kind of love does not corrupt by appealing to the ego; rather, it tends to correct egotism by rebuking the prideful nature of others.

The more corrupt and bizarre the cultural hero is, the

closer to the source of evil he (or she) must be, and the greater the emotional shock-value generated in the faithless undead. The lower people sink, the lower the corrupter has to sink to stay ahead, to shock the undead into believing in their accursed eternal life.

The more wrong we become, the more energy we are *compelled* to give our comforter/corrupters. We simply must confer greatness upon people to amplify their ability to stimulate what we think of as life. We make them omnipotent and then, emotionally caught up in the delirium of pleasure and pain, we cannot see where all our miseries are coming from—them!

To become a leader, an ambitious man is obliged to play a female's role. Playing friend and humble servant, seductive men weaken the people and take power in exactly the same way that whores and guileful women do. Appearing to hold the people's best interest at heart, power-hungry business, medical, political and religious psychopaths and their cohort psychotics conspire to bleed the nation of its money and vitality. When trouble results, the experts gravely stroke their beards concerning all the symptoms, never addressing themselves to the *cause* (of which they are a part), and that is why their ego-consoling or aggravating cures are always worse than the disease.

The government points to inflation and asks us to hold the line on prices while it is printing money. Doctors point to germs as the cause of disease while they are drugging us, irradiating us and slicing us up, sending us to the grave on the installment plan. The detective, as it were, turns out to be the murderer—and he is the last to be suspected because he hides behind the laws you need to protect you from the effects of the temptation of the other, criminal kind of psychopath. The people are all caught between the psychopaths who want to make them wrong on one hand, and those who claim to make them right on the other.

Through greed and hypocrisy, sly, subhuman psychopaths, both social and criminal, set the stage for the inevitable economic holocaust, depression and rebellion. When detection time arrives, the only way social psychopaths can prevent revolution and hold the nation together is by a threat to the common welfare—so then we go to war. Guileful women often use the same tactics to hold the loyalty of their weak men.

The evil spirit in people often creates for them imaginary enemies to fight so that it (the corrupt "government" in them) is not detected. That kind of distraction is called paranoia in the individual. The pathological manifestations of it at its worst are cancer and war. When the wicked king sends soldiers against the revolutionaries, it would appear that the king is attacking the enemy of society; however, there would *be* no enemy if the king were just.

Preceding war and revolution, the leaders—those dominant, part-male, part-female, part-devil social psychopaths—bring into existence two "sons." One of them is the conformist who enjoys "mommy's" favor—you know, positions of authority and high-paying jobs as rewards for copping out. The other is the rebel "son" who hates his nanny-leaders and his spoiled, momma-centered, characterless brother who won't see what is wrong with his mother (King Kong with bloomers on) and all the rest of the whores in charge of home and society.

214

The psychotics of any culture are in general loved, dominated and exploited by a legion of seductive, smiling leaders who gain power by lie-loving the people. After tempting to gain power, they show their true nature, exploiting addiction through taxes, alcohol, music, tobacco, religion, medicine and a host of other seductive, ego-supportive comforts that assuage the guilt of the culture. Then when a Hitler or a Charles Manson type comes along to champion the rebel cause, the evil, which once worked more secretly and slyly in the morbid, plastic social order, is unleashed through a psychopathic revolutionary head who then leads us into the more obvious horrors of a dictatorship.

The spirit of hypocrisy in any democracy sets the stage for chaos and for evil to arise out of the pit through the matrix of the weak-charactered masses. The psychotic masses, you see, always express the will of the strongest influence.

Responding as they do to the most dominant influence, the slimy, conforming, lily-livered, psychotic, sinful masses who once copped out to momma can be counted on to do the murderous bidding of their new leader. Yet evil doesn't have to come in the form of a Hitler or a Charles Manson—the bloody history of religious purges will show you what a thin mask hypocrisy is for wickedness. You could marry someone reassuring who seems to love you—and then one day a monster emerges who cleans you out, makes your life a misery and nags you to death.

The home is the microcosm of this satanic female-dictator principle. The pyramid of corrupt families which makes up the nation is its macrocosm. The people represent the weak father and son who love to be seduced and spoiled by the leader-wife-mother who excites them into a sense of omnipotence and self-righteousness while really making their lives miserable.

No matter how little authority they are given, few people can resist the temptation to use it to play God, to condemn or to lift others to all the highs of new lows. And the more authority, the greater is the temptation to be an evil god. Absolute power corrupts the ambitious absolutely. The quickest way to power and glory lies through deception, but, as a psychopath, this means that you must become a vehicle for evil. On the other hand, to give up that quest for power, to disarm yourself, is to become an instrument, a vessel of the truth which is from God, as the lie is from the devil.

There is a sinister spirit operating everywhere through the fanfare and tinsel of tradition. The so-called "good folks" of society *need* the criminal element they have projected to complement their "goodness." Both systems of evil—hypocrisy and dictatorship—are threatened by truth and innocence. The so-called good folks are the first to crucify Messiah and to cry, "Give us Barabbas!"

In every family which has been corrupted by the system, regardless of whether it is a hypocrisy or a dictatorship, the prevailing rule is this: *to confuse, to confound and to make a lie the truth and the truth a lie in order for evil to hold on to its usurped power and false righteousness.* For if the innocent can be made to doubt themselves, if sensitive children can be destroyed, driven mad and stuck in mental hospitals and jails, then everyone, including the hierarchy of psychopathic exploiters, is safe from detection.

216

Remember, there are two ways of forcing people to doubt the truth: one way is by praising, "loving" and accepting them just as they are. Where that fails, they can be pressured and degraded with cruelty so as to create obedience through their resentment.

In business, you see both kinds of dictators. One is the weak, effeminate man who knows how to get the most for the least by being an all-things-to-all-people, "loving" type. Then you have the despicable, unprincipled-dog type of supervisor—he too can get the efficient most-for-the-least by browbeating and motivating. And both of these criminals have the power to reinforce the hell in their victims.

Freud was right when he said that people are rarely moved except by conflict. When praise is accepted, it sets up conflict too, and we move to ease such pressure by appeasement. Between being praised and being downgraded, we are totally enslaved, and we become addicted to our corrupters.

There are three types of people who develop within the framework of the plastic concentration camps (homes, factories and offices) of a hypocrisy/democracy.

The first kind of zombie, you remember, is the conformist, hated by his brother, the rebel. The conformist is confused; he believes his weakness is goodness because the system that created him rewards him for it. This proud, self-righteous one does not see his greed and the confounding inconsistencies of his own life. He picks a wife just like momma and, as a weak father himself, sires another brood of rebels and conformists. He can't see how his phony religion, medicine and causes, just like his momma and his wife, lie-comfort him to death. Unconsciously,

217

he elects the supportive momma in all his political "choices," too.

The rebel rejects all the traditional values, even when they are sound. He is on the outside what his mother, father and brothers are on the inside—full of hate and wickedness.

Hypocrisy projects a monster which hatches out in the rebel and seeks revenge upon the momma Frankenstein and the society which created it. The number of these psychotic monsters is growing daily, and they are just waiting for a leader to arise to love them just as they are, as Hitler did the Nazis, to reward the overt expression of their pent-up, vile, animal spirit. When that time comes, you will see another world order of horror, another holocaust set in motion by hypocrisy.

The rebel type kills overtly without pity or pretense, while the hypocrite will steal from you and then kill you very subtly, as though he were somehow doing you a favor.

The third group of people who are born subject to the hell-world of culture consists of men and women like you and me. We, too, are infected by the spirit of hypocrisy and violence, and we, too, project confusion in our offspring, making them doubt themselves in order to satisfy the hellfire which burns inside us. But the difference is that we don't like the way we are. We can realize the truth, and we would be willing to change if we could only find the way out of bondage.

Even inside us, evil is defensive against good. The sickness which has made a home in you (with or without your agreement) defends itself by confusing others about what they see in you. Because we are all born slaves, subject to sin, the indwelling evil inherently has the power to make others doubt themselves. So with this one-upsmanship authority, the indwelling evil in us succeeds in projecting and in corrupting and sustaining others, and so it maintains the upper hand. It sows and projects rebellion and conformity, the two extremes of madness, into succeeding generations, which continue to evolve one another and to destroy one another in multitudinous feuds, purges and wars.

People who hate authority are guilty because hatred is a wrong reaction, and their guilt makes them need support. So they set up their own authority to help them soothe the pain of their guilt, and here they become enslaved again.

It is hard to hold on to your sanity in this mad, irrational world, but you must. The time is coming soon when evil's rule will be exposed for what it is. It begins for you with the reading of these words.

It is a blessing to admit when you are wrong. The more you know when you are wrong (and repent), the more surely you know it when you are right, because both are based on truth. There is a right and a wrong way of believing in yourself. You don't want to believe in yourself when you are wrong, and neither should others believe in you if that is the case.

Your duty is to come to the light, repent and believe in what you had left behind. With new insight, surety and strength, you must make the entire wicked world doubt the sanity of its insanity. You owe it to the prisoners (not the willing slaves) of the system to help free them from their bondage to sin (which came about through their doubting of the truth) by making them doubt the lie.

Do not be disturbed if others think you are cruel and

cold because your honesty exposes them to their own confusion and agony—*better that their kind cry and die than our kind.* For if there were a choice between keeping silent and speaking truly, thereby driving the entire world mad except for one single person who, hearing it, might be saved, you ought to speak boldly and save just that one. All who remain are worthless garbage in the eyes of heaven. The wicked and prideful have been made to *feel* worthy through lies and liars, to which they cling. Living under a curse, they fear the light of their own conscience and they also fear your coming to the light. Their hatred of good, and their love of evil (as good) is an addiction from which there is no salvation. Verily, they have their (false) salvation.

Pride drops dead in the light of reality. The world will make you feel wrong for holding fast to what is right. You will no doubt come to know what it means to be persecuted for righteousness' sake. But the reason why you will feel so wrong is that your former "righteousness" was based upon pleasing and judging wicked people. Back in the neutral zone where there is no hate or "love," your own soul is bared to the truth of its past sins. So when the world withdraws its support to "punish" you for your disloyalty, you may feel the guilt you never felt before. That is a good thing! Salvation comes only to those who welcome the purging pain of guilt by giving up the security of emotion based on loving and hating and believing the lie.

Seeing evil as evil, you shrink from it, and that is like believing *into* God. To believe the truth about evil is to be saved from its power of deception. After all, didn't Adam doubt God's word when he believed the serpent about becoming like God himself? And is not seeking reassurance for this wrong what your problems are all about? And who was it who said, "You shall know the truth, and the truth shall make you free"?

The Truth, ever-present as a Light who does not speak, reveals error as error only to those who seek Him. Everywhere, people are lost in the comforting, velvety darkness. Lost in the hypnosis of sin where there is no light to reveal the error, to make them repent, they cannot be saved.

Only a true belief can counter a false belief. Until the light of true belief is welcome, you remain at the mercy of satanic suggestion. The light does not reveal what is in the darkness if you *hide* in the darkness. If the comfort of doubt's darkness makes you feel secure from the light, you remain an enemy of the light, a tormented pawn of hell whose only delight is to put out the light in your fellows.

But if you are one of the few who welcome the light which illumines these words in your heart, *then see evil as evil, wrong as wrong (without puffing up in judgment) and never again doubt the wordless knowing within.* See how you have become an emotional slave of the lie through its appeal to your selfishness and greed. Observe its way of discrediting values and morality to free you from conscience.

You must discover how to deal with your problems *without feeling.* You must seek that special neutral zone, that space in your mind where you can move and have your being without the stuff that beasts and demons are made of—without animal love and hate. Only then, armed with true compassion, can you defeat the spirit of temptation in all its disguises.

221

The spiritual light which speaks to you without words is like the light from the sun to the eye. As the sun is to the eye, so is the light to the soul (by which the soul discerns all things clearly so that it does not stumble). The light is ever-present. The light has always been with you, but your ego, adventuring into past and future imagery, could neither perceive it nor receive it. Instead, you were like a blind man guided in the night by a deceptive voice that spoke through your intellect, directing, excusing and comforting you in every folly, which seemed like the voice of your own true conscience urging you toward a glorious destiny. Now that you know that it was a lie, you may begin your journey to the light, the Truth who can make you free.

12 Death Wish

There are many ways to die, but none of them are the will of the Creator; they are instead the projection of the unconscious death wish of the victim. And when our will is not God's will, it is really the extension of Satan's purpose, which is to draw our souls to himself.

The majority of people feel that they are dealing with their problems when they are really only dealing with the "problem" of reality. The prideful answers they seek require dealing with the *awareness* of whatever they see is wrong with themselves, and that, in metaphysical terms, is tantamount to the rejection of God.

God's truth has the power to save everyone from sickness, tragedy and death, providing, of course, that each one is willing to realize the error of his ways. Regretfully, it is not the nature of the prideful person to be sorry for anything—therefore does the soul, consumed by pride, perish.

There is no accident, no horror, no suffering that comes by chance. Each person who perishes is under a spell as part of an infernal plan—a destiny, if you like. But up to the point of no return, we have the opportunity to change our destiny any time we wish to wake up.

When the positive force of faith disintegrates through greed and doubt, then do the vile and violent negative forces rush in to fill the void. Where there is no divine order there is chaos, just as where there is no true democracy there appears a climate of horror, inhumanity and death.

It is integrity and faith which provide a shield of protection against the law of evil destiny. You cannot see the laws of nature, but you can see their effects manifested in the whole of creation. Similarly, obedience or disobedience to the laws written in the heart of man manifests a lifestyle. Depending on the degree to which the laws of the state conform to moral law, we bring into being a Hitler Germany, a cannibal kingdom or the U.S.A.

Let us examine the idea of destiny by looking at the following example: a sleepwalker is poised at the edge of a cliff as someone shouts a warning. What is his reaction? If he awakens and is grateful for the warning, he steps back out of danger. But if he instead pursues his dream and refuses to hear, he is lost. If he hears the warning and awakens in time but resents knowing the truth about his situation, he will be drawn into the yawning chasm, pulled in by the magnetic force of his own fascination and fear.

Then what can this writer say to this perverse generation? What does it take to awaken the psychotic sleepwalking masses?

Recognizing a potential problem, you might say to a friend, "Stay away from that person. She (or he) is no good for you. She will ruin your life. Don't marry, for goodness' sake!" But your friend cannot see the tragedy ahead because he is seeking some kind of selfish advantage (which he perceives as happiness), and that blinds him to the reality of the situation.

And although you may not be involved with that particular kind of fascination, you no doubt have warning signals about your own problems which you ignore. You may be smoking, overeating or drinking, and you may have a friend who is trying to tell you, but you won't listen. "I only live once," you think to yourself. Or, "This is one of my few pleasures, one of the nice things I do for myself." You have fabricated many excuses that make your own folly seem innocent, even beneficial. "If one has to go anyway," you tell yourself, "overeating is surely a pleasant way to do it. And sex! What a way to die! After all, you can't live forever! Right?" Wrong!

Most, if not all, of your comforts are really little bits of death. Each little vice doubles as an escape and an ego reinforcement, a traumatic means by which your ego seems to grow and cope with the "problem"—reality. Each indulgence is a secret means by which the painful awareness of folly is set aside.

Pride is at the root of all our problems. So you see, it is really impossible to deal with any problem from an egocentric state of mind, because what appears as the problem is itself simply a manifestation of the willful, hell-centered ego. The only way pride knows to deal with its own problem is to deal with the reality that shows it to *be* a problem. Then enters that strategic ego-reinforcing, distracting comfort, and evil becomes our waiter, entertainer and lover.

If it is true that *dis-ease* is caused by the soul's rejection of truth, surely it should be easy to see that the soul which rejected truth in the first place (and thus created the problem) can be stubborn enough to reject it a second and third time. In this way the soul goes on compounding the problem by rejecting the reality of it, until it reaches a point of no return. Nearly all the way up to that point you have an alternative, a way out—but only if you wake up in time to follow that option provided by waking up. To accept the true answer, you must reject your old solutions. The *old* securities have to go.

Look, what do you do if your car breaks down? Surely you open the hood and look inside to see what went wrong. But if you don't have any mechanical know-how, how is the problem going to be revealed? Without a standard against which to contrast the problem, your engine just looks like a pile of guts and spaghetti.

In going your own prideful way, in your failure to find God through trying to be God yourself, you have set aside the unique kind of knowing that reveals what your problem is. It is like this: if you don't know you are wrong, you think everything is all right, and so you go on to make a bigger mess as you try to "fix your engine" without understanding why it broke down.

Your ego, consumed by pride, has not wanted to face the truth. Understanding has always been a pain that threatened the integrity of your egocentricity. To survive, your stubborn ego has reacted resentfully and defensively against realizing the truth. For a season, you lived a "charmed" life because any time you wished, you could refuse to look at the evidence and make the problem go away. On the strength of the false security provided by your comforts, you were able to go on believing in your own prideful future. You then had the false hope and confidence that all egos have when truth is not present to show the futility of their existence.

Resentment, like the vice it is, has the power to keep you safely and psychotically asleep regardless of whether it is resentment against conscience (which is like a friend warning you and trying to awaken you to the awful reality), or whether it is just plain resentment toward people, past or present. Remember that resentment is the classic ego-survival defense mechanism. Through resentment you produce a psychotic state of false security, but because that adds sin to sin, the pain that follows increases the need for pleasure. Although pleasure helps you escape guilt feelings, it also enslaves and frustrates. That in turn threatens you and provides additional grounds for hostility. After you have lost (or rejected) everything, all you have left is hate to keep you in your self-righteous psychotic state.

When one deals with experiences correctly, one never ever has to reexperience them, not mentally or physically. Past errors are only repeated because you *resent* being reminded of and awakened to the knowledge of sin in you which all memories contain. Who was it who said that those who refuse to learn from history are doomed to reexperience it?

You deeply *resent* memories which remind you of your past failures to deal with a succession of psychopaths (who all remain alive and well inside you). The more conflict you develop through failure, the more guilt stains your soul, and the more you fear and resent awakening to reality. You remain asleep through the vice of "loving" and the vice of hating. You may even grow to hate that which you once "loved," because you were hurt by that experience.

All failure is due to the collapse of faith and wisdom through a successful appeal to the ego. Once the force field of faith collapses, lawless error rushes in. You experience it, it becomes you, and you become the instrument of its destiny for you. However, because you are not facing reality, you may not see those factors that go on working through you to destroy your life. Perceiving the danger can be your protection. Therefore, take heed! Take another good look at this thing called love, which amounts to clinging to people, places or things for security. And also look at hate and the psychotic ecstasy of blame and judgment which it provides.

If you can believe what I have said (but you can't until you are ready to stop being prideful), then you are ready to be saved from taking the next step toward death and hell.

The time to decide you don't like the military is *not* in the face of the enemy; it is sometime before that point. Preferably, you avoid joining up in the first place. To get out safely down the line is progressively more dangerous. Consider the airplane pilot who, from the time he taxies along the runway to the time he lifts off, has options about taking off. There is a point of no return when, like it or not, he must take to the air.

Life is similar. You have many opportunities to choose as you go down life's road, but it is much easier on you to wake up early and live by the eternal rather than the infernal system of choices. The way gets tougher as you near the end. Then there comes the inevitable point of no return and you are dead, dead because you were stubborn in your disbelief of the truth.

You can either believe in what *is* so, or in what is *not*

so. Attached to each type of belief there is a reward: either an accursed eternal life as a god (in hell) or a blessed eternal life as a child of God. Satan offered Adam eternal life if he would doubt God so as to become God himself, but God told Adam he would die if he tried it. Adam paid for his sin with death. Many who inherit death as part of the life of pride prefer not to see death as punishment for sin, but rather as a door to eternal life. Their pride still looks to knowledge to save them from the sin of looking to the knowledge tree. They simply cannot believe the truth about death, for to see the truth about death would force them to admit the sin of pride and to give pride up.

The life that leads to death is like going through a door through a door through a door, with something shimmering like an eternal fountain waiting beyond each threshold. As each door slams shut behind, what shimmered and beckoned is seen for what it is—a prison within a prison within a prison. The last door, the very last ego escape to glory, is death. And beyond death is the ultimate experience of "heavenly" hell. And all the way down, to preserve your pride, you keep rejecting the truth about what is happening to you.

In spite of all the tragedies, diseases and sufferings you experience, you persist in hungering for and clinging to the things which frustrate and breed the dependency you call love. You tend to adhere more tenaciously than ever to your possessions, cultures, vices and admirers for the familiar psychotic form of security they provide. They allow you to think in a way you should not; through them you keep hoping vainly for the best. Your infernal salvation hangs in the balance and you will "bust your gut" forcing hell to make good its promise.

Many Jewish people in Nazi Germany refused to see what was happening around them. They could not believe their eyes. The egocentric ones kept clinging and hoping for the best until it was too late. "It will be all right," they told themselves. Pride made them cling to their ego-securities, their homes and businesses. The worse things became, the harder it was to face up to reality. And the way they dealt with the horror around them was to disbelieve the *reality* of it by clinging to their possessions until all they had was hate, and then it was too late to do anything. Only a remnant could see what was coming and fled to safety. Saved by perception, these people heeded the warnings of their conscience. Even so, there is yet another level of responding to conscience that can go on to save your soul as well as your body. Moses saved men from Egypt. Christ saves men from the bondage of sin and death.

Prior to World War II, Winston Churchill said, "If you will not fight for right when you can easily win without bloodshed, then you will have to fight when there is no chance for victory."

The type of salvation the foolish soul chooses is saving face. Any degrading psychotic pleasure or pain experience can dull the agony of anxiety, helping us to set aside the awareness of reality. That is why the threshold to each debilitating movement downward looks more and more inviting to the surviving ego, *even when the experience is one of sheer terror.*

Remember, the prideful person must remain asleep at all costs to avoid seeing his own mistakes; and if he is to sleep, he must dream. When the psychotic dream which pleasure provides gives way to reveal the wickedness behind it, all the victim has left to escape into is the nightmare psychosis produced by terror. Instead of waking up, the ego uses the hatred of evil to provide escape from seeing its own wrong, just as it once used the pleasures provided by its love of evil for escape. We employ evil when we love it, and again when we hate it, and we are enslaved to it both ways.

Death occurs basically because of the debilitating excitement of judgment. The wicked one, in providing food for your secret judgment, shocks you into a psychotic, omnipotent fantasy state. You get high through loving what loves you and then later through hating what hates you. You fail to realize, of course, that through every love/hate judgment you are actually using evil to reject reality and to preserve your own sense of being that reality.

Unwittingly, we perpetuate the original sin. We cloud our minds and involve our egos with escape through selfish pleasure. Through interreacting with pleasure and pain, we are able to reinforce the glory-bound, faithless, psychotic sleepwalking state of original sin, edging ever closer to the very sickness, horror, tragedy and death we are trying to forget or deny. *Tragedy always enters through our rejection of truth. There is only one solution: stand and face reality; otherwise, you must try to cure the tragedy by denying the reality of it, and that effort is doomed to fail.*

Once the ego-animal evolution begins, you fear losing your reassuring pleasure/pain securities, which trigger and reinforce ego hopes and dreams. You fear letting go of sustaining evils. Your ego fears awakening and "dying" in the light. Think of it—you actually fear that you will die if you give up your resentments and comforts.

You can (and usually do) transfer the authority and power that your corrupters have to sustain your ego life to some object which affects you the same way people do. You do this to avoid seeing the terrible power others have over you while still enjoying the reinforcing "benefits" of their presence.

Let us say someone pushes you into the water and you cannot swim. It is possible to fear and resent the water as a way of taking away the realization of your humiliation. If you don't *see* that you hate the person who humiliated and degraded you, you can go *on* using him secretly as a hate object without feeling guilty about it or seeing your enslavement to him.

Remember the rule of corruption, which is: you need reinforcing love or hate from the corrupting source. Your ego survives on shock: the shock of loving evil and hating it. Furthermore, you can transfer your hatred from one thing to another to distract yourself from the guilt of the previous hate.

The corrupted have a weird fascination with the sick spirit of their corrupter. You see this sort of thing happening to hostages who have lived under extreme terror. Evil, whether it is in the form of a pleasurable or an obviously unpleasant experience, has power to infuse into you the infernal identity of pride. People actually fall into a debilitating, dependent love with their corrupters. Reveling in what seems to be a vital reinforcing experience, many are drawn to lower and lower levels of evil like flies to dung. Whether it be a seductive woman who becomes a tyrant, a government that becomes a tyrant, or an amiable rogue whose trauma-inducing presence relieves us of guilt and makes us feel "loved," the reinforcing evil spirit behind it all is the same.

Your sin-based identity is forever drawn hypnotically to the false security provided by your corrupters. We are always defrauded by those who tease us with Satan's ancient promise of infernal life.

Let me rub this in again by saying that it is *you* who give power to evil people to excite you into forgetfulness and a sense of independent eternal growth. So consequently, what develops in, through and around you is sin, which must again be forgotten. As long as you have a need to play God, you will also have a need for a means to forget the sin of it. You want to be safe in your psychotic reality where, for one infernal moment, you are not wrong, you are God. And for this trick, you need a psychopathic someone or something to cling to, to excite you into feeling secure and omnipotent.

When we are challenged by wickedness and try to evolve above it by becoming greater than it, *we* are it. If we are not able to overcome it and we remain a victim, then we use the cruelty to keep us in an omnipotent trance of judgment. We may try appeasement as a way of compelling evil to be good. We bend over backwards trying to manipulate the wickedness into giving us the supporting love our kingly egos crave; but that is precisely what gives people power to be even more wicked to us. Our egos are served by evil whether we are enslaved to its cruelty or its pleasures, because we need its hypnotic power to keep us asleep to reality.

The variety of ways in which people deny reality and die is mind boggling. The most dangerous, because they seem the most innocent and natural, are food and sex.

No question about it—one can literally sex and eat oneself into the grave, perhaps while grunting, "What a way to die!"

By now you should see what I mean when I say that man is no ordinary animal. He is an animal, but only through the fault of pride. Unlike ordinary animals, he is *unnaturally* natural. Contemporary man is not created the way man was originally. Because man is now born of woman, of the lineage of original sin (pride), it is easy for him to forget or to misconstrue the truth about how he was originally created to exist in an earthly paradisiacal state and how he came down from that existence to the pigsty jungle he presently wallows in.

Every descendent of original sin has two natures and two origins, referred to earlier in this text. Within us, our inherited carnal nature wars for ascendency against the spiritual potential which was once man's birthright.

One part of you cries, "Give in to your natural feelings. Stop pretending to be something you can't be. Be good to yourself. Reward yourself. Enjoy life!" The snake in your gut persuades you that your guilts and conflicts are caused by not being honest enough to give in to your true (lower) nature. Indeed, there *is* a struggle going on; but experience should have already proven that to give in to the carnal nature results in greater conflict. The tendency of the soul is toward awakening and realizing the error of its ways; conflict results when this process is unwelcome. Look again at how your ego inherently defends itself against guilt by running toward the evil comfort of a psychotic, culture-oriented crutch. *Comfort is ego-sustaining, just as it is an escape.* It is the trapdoor through which the inhuman identity enters.

234

The mortal animal-self evidences our heritage of original sin. The life-support systems to it are food and sex. That is why you begin to feel hungers and lusts whenever you are teased and tempted to fall. The two strongest desires are to eat (survive) and to procreate. When these appetites are aroused by your failure to cope, you feel a vague embarrassment (modesty), which increases according to your ignorance of its meaning in terms of your origin. Your growing anxiety allows you to be upset, aggravated and teased even more, and consequently the sensual appetite increases to the point where you can be controlled through people toying with your senses.

How have you always dealt with embarrassment as you reached the threshold of understanding about your origin? Did you not again and again deal with your self-consciousness by dealing with the *awareness* itself? Did you not abandon yourself to sensuality for relief? Identifying with the animal self, you forgot your anxiety, but only for a while. Later, when you saw the folly of it, you struggled angrily with your sensuality and tried to repress it, and that made things worse.

Mortal appetites evolve through prideful responses, and whether they are indulged or repressed, they rise to be observed again and again. When we stubbornly doubt the truth of what is plain to see and thus God's pleasure in us ceases, there is left for us only the unholy comfort in, or struggle against, our hang-ups.

More than anything, the male ego wants to be wanted. He feels that he is not a man unless he is accepted by a woman. (It is true that a male is not a whole man, but his condition can never be cured by having a woman.) At the slightest hint of acceptance, his failing (represented by sex) is turned around and seen as a virtue. To the fallen man, such adventures seem like a movement forward to life and happiness, a way of becoming a more glorious super-being. Tobacco, alcohol, drugs, sex and food remove the feeling that something is wrong by setting aside the awareness of the wrong observed.

I am not speaking here about ordinary sex or ordinary eating. I refer here only to sex and eating as they are used for comfort and ego-escape. To escape is to add sin to sin; to escape is to reinforce the animal and to take pride in the animal, and thus to strengthen the ancient covenant with hell and death.

The original lie-appeal to man's ego changed his body through his altered consciousness. Acceptance of the gross and sensual man is the seducer's way of helping the victim doubt that anything is wrong with himself and his pride. The sustaining lie generates more false confidence and thus more ego-sensuality; that is why it all seems like growing. When we are accepted for our faults or perversions, it adds sin to sin, and each one of those experiences is a little bit of death that seems like life.

To accept any lie, no matter how small, is to reject the truth. As your ego accepts the lie, it forms a stronger bond with the deceiving instrument so that you come more and more to share its evil destiny, death. Escaping and identifying with the lie and the flesh (which is aroused by the deceiver), you lose the ability to see deeply as you were meant to; you see only as beasts do, and you are controlled like beasts. Your refusal to see what is wrong renders you a helpless slave to the process of deception.

Gentlemen, consider this if you will: the woman who pretends to worship and crave your genitals, making you feel wanted, important and manly, is without exception *a vampirish, parasitical harpie who loves the power she gets from promoting your weakness.* Beware of being honored by a female's clinging, by her hungering for your body's substance. Soon you will become impotent and lifeless. And somewhere in between here and there you will be driven to alcohol, drugs, or to those other "understanding" women to save you from the last demanding bitch who was eating you alive. Think of such love and your fascination with it as a vampire/zombie relationship. It is hypnotically irresistible because of the ego need for infernal eternal-life reassurance as part and parcel of romance. As you are bitten and stricken, you become one of the undead, learning to live on others as others live from you.

Down you go through those sexual, eating, drinking, smoking, musical doors to the darker dungeons of the lower realms. You try to get out, as an escaping dreamer seeks answers in deeper dreams rather than the true answer of waking up from the dream. I tell you the truth: it is Satan who is in charge, who reaches out to meet you in your dreaming; all roads lead to his dark light at the end of the infernal tunnel.

I don't want to go into the endless variations of sin, because there would be no end to writing. But let me emphasize that the woman who enslaves you and becomes a tormenting, demanding witch has the qualities you, sir, have cultivated because of your psychotic ego-need to be elevated by her devilish, sustaining "love." The lie in her is what you admired, got excited by and married her for. Madly in love, you encouraged her to debilitate and destroy you, and you wallowed like a pig in

237

every minute of it. How were you to know you were teaching her how to suck on you and bleed you dry in exchange for the false ego-security of psychotic bliss? Apply this principle on a global scale to any relationship you care to mention, and behold, you will see God's perfect justice for the sinning masses. They are all tortured to death by the very people they elect to pump up their ailing pride.

Comfort is reassuring because it removes the feeling that something is wrong. You are addicted to the idea that all is well, and that is the lie which kills. A lying lover sucks on your weakness as though you were a candy bar, a sweet and wonderful person. And instead of seeing yourself being degraded, you feel uplifted. You don't see that you are being eaten alive; you think you are being loved. All psychotic souls enjoy being degraded and poisoned by their pleasures, because through them they can continue to doubt that they are wrong. Those who are never wrong are gods.

Remember what I said about the two ways of living eternally. One of them is to repent of the sin of pride. The other is to pridefully reaffirm that you already *have* eternal life, believing that your only guilt comes from not fully accepting that you are God.

None of the big, fat, ugly, cancerous females and the red-nosed, pot-bellied, drinking degenerates see their ugliness, the mess they have made of their lives, so long as they munch, drink and sex merrily away. While you are eating that turkey leg or guzzling that jug of whiskey, you are forgetting your ugliness. You experience yourself as a beautiful being, getting the most out of living, and you think, "Man, this is the life!"

Every time you dunk yourself in pleasure (or pain),

you reinforce the ancient aspiration of pride to be God, living forever. For a fleeting moment, as long as the indulgence lingers, you forget reality and feel you are a step closer to getting the devil to make good his promise. For another fleeting moment, you are saved from the pain of truth. In this manner, you waste your substance bit by bit until you come to the final morning after the night before.

Evil is seen only as contrasted by the revealing light. Sensual experiences tend to remove awareness by gluing or fusing the soul to the flesh. As beasts, we cease being perceptive; we do not see our evil mentors for what they are because we must use their services to help us lose sight of what good is. All the while, the wicked shepherd rubs his hands with glee. His vampirish nature enjoys degrading us, introducing us to his many infernal delights, delusions and judgments, and thence to his suffering. We are degraded when we indulge in his pleasures and again when, led like donkeys, we are delivered up to his wrath. If our soul cannot resist his vampirish pleasure, neither can we escape his cruelty. For every moment of escape, there are a thousand moments of suffering.

At each point along the way, decadence is reinforced as we become more and more centered in evil through escape into sensual experience. As truth becomes ever more painful to our souls, sin seems more attractive. The lower we sink, the more vile things appeal to us, drawing us further away from reality toward the infernal "life giving" evil through the improper polarity of our souls.

The traditional comforts of home are nearly always escapes from reality. You are actually killing yourselves and one another with your excesses as your pride stubbornly prefers the salvation of sensation to the salvation of sense. Middle age is that time of life when you would do anything to get well, except give up what is killing you.

Remember that to the ego, the death wish appears as gusto for life. It may not be easy to detect at first, but every deceiving comfort carries with it Satan's ancient promise of eternal life. The psychopath's vampirish lure is irresistible to his zombie sinner. When this "love" bug bites, your ego is injected with the venom of Satan's own undying nature, the accursed, undying life of pride.

But when you cleave to what is true, preferring the understanding about sin to the experience of it, then you will die to the infernal life (death) and come alive eternally in God. Either way, whether you are moving from death to life or from life to death, you experience the dichotomy of feeling as if you are dying and living at the same time. Wake up, if you will, and let your inherited death wish (the desire for infernal eternal life in you) be replaced by the life wish—your desire for God's will in you.

13 The Power of Perception

To see things clearly, as they are, to perceive with understanding in a wordless way—to have common sense—is a gift. That perfect energy state of knowing and being provided power and guidance to the ancient wise men. They called it *the light*. The light gave Moses the power to stand up to Pharaoh.

We must all be Moses and Jesus types, or else perish. The indwelling light is a "lamp unto your feet." Where there is light and power, there is no need to worry, to scheme and to plan your way through life.

For most of the people in this world, the light has gone out. As creatures of darkness, they move and have their being by the eerie luminescence of their imaginations. They may look like us, talk like us and act like us, but they are not coming from the same place. There is available to those of us who love the truth the power to see what is wrong with ourselves and the world, and so we can change everything for the better. But they cannot. Because they hate the light and therefore must try to put it out, they cannot perceive circumstances clearly or realistically. Believing that they are making a better world, they destroy themselves and those around them, and then they "save" themselves by not seeing where the fault lies.

It is the ambitious ones who fear the light. You can tell who they are whenever you wheel the conversation around to meaningful subject matter. They become antagonistic when you speak of moral issues and thereby threaten their secret lifestyle. They react defensively to you the way they react against their own conscience.

These imperfect people exist on the imperfect energy triggered by intrigue, pressure and sensual pleasures. They enjoy being stressed and, like the vultures they are, they in turn take special delight in degrading and pressuring those around them.

While we may also react to and take our identity from pressure, compulsively taking our hostilities out on the less fortunate, we find no joy in it. We are troubled to receive such a nature and to live under the dog-eat-dog order of challenge and animal growth. We may indeed inherit the same kind of destructive habits—alcohol, tobacco, or drugs, for example—but try as we will, we cannot enjoy indulging ourselves as others do. And let us not forget the degenerative diseases, the problems with job, children, finances and marriage which arise from our wrong reaction to pressure. We who love the truth cannot be satisfied with the usual "answers" from worldly authorities who rise out of the slimy pit of iniquity to serve and soothe our wounded egos.

It may not seem as though we have anything special, but we do. The darkness people sense it, and they react to what we cannot see working in our midst. Offended, they may treat us as though we were contaminated dirt.

Nevertheless, we are very special people, chosen from the beginning of time for a special destiny. Remember the story of the ugly duckling who was really a beautiful swan? That is you and me.

Even though you may now be confused, from the day of your birth you were blessed with the potential ability to understand about people and things without being taught. You have always potentially had the power to make effortless, sensible, meaningful decisions; to run your affairs with wisdom; to understand; to love; to prosper; to build a paradise on earth as easily as a sparrow builds her nest. And what is more important, you have the power to prevail over evil, to project and establish every day, each in your own way, a little bit of the kingdom of heaven on earth. That is precisely why they mock, hate and fear you. You see, the light which shines in you bares their souls and reveals their hell-bound nature.

The light, exposing the folly of pride, burns. The light has a way of forbidding and shattering dreams, goals and images, making wickedness doubt itself. Your light acts as an external conscience to others which both shames and inhibits the lifestyle that rises through pride's dreams.

Cunning and willfulness become impotent in the presence of innocence. Believing, seeing and shining as you do disables the vainglorious schemes of others from hatching out on earth as they do in hell.

Belief is the secret catalyst to any kind of achievement, whether it be good or evil. Faith in the light makes people doubt their false beliefs. But those who cling to deception are desperate people, and in order to believe in themselves, they *must* make you doubt the truth.

Until you fully understand your ultimate destiny you

are, to some degree, a product of their world and subject to their slavish feudal system. But your heart is different from theirs—you are glad to realize where you have gone wrong. You are seeking the truth you lost through the persistence of your persecutors, which found its mark through your ignorance and faithlessness.

Those villains actually want to kill you! And the chief destroyer is most often likely to be a member of your own immediate family—your mother, father, brother or sister. Although you may not have met me personally, the spirit that writes these words is much more family than your own flesh and blood.

Your sin was the classic error of believing there was something wrong with you for seeing something wrong with the villains around you. That caused you to step across to their life (protesting, perhaps) to become like them. Now that you have seen the error, you don't know how to get back. You are resentful.

The first step is to realize the error of your original doubt. Also see that resentment and blame is what is keeping you in that trap. People got your goat because there was a goat to get. You had to learn the lesson of pride before you could come to God.

Return as a little child. What you once had was (and still is) the truth, which when trusted and obeyed through faith becomes power to affect the wicked world.

What you now have, making you wretched, is doubt. When your mind has a single faith, your whole body is full of light. But the double-minded person (double means being of two minds) is unstable.

He who does not answer to enlightened reason exists under the power of evil.

You see, the enlightened reason forbids the evolutionary growth of pride apart from God to be God yourself. Incorrigible egos cannot give up their earthy experiences which challenge and stimulate them to growth as God. They may give up their lives, but they will not give up those experiences upon which their ego securities rest.

Whether you end up murdered or die in a car crash, of disease or in war, makes little difference. Sooner or later the laws of sin, change and decay will claim you. It may seem as if our destiny is a matter of chance, but that is only because pride prevents us from seeing the inevitable consequences of our actions. The prideful nature, which is nourished by excitement, plays a lifelong game of Russian roulette with death, and the only element of "chance" involved is that we do not know which chamber the bullet is in.

During the formative period of their fallen existence, the (yet spiritually unborn) children of light are protected from death, though they may be drawn in to the quicksand of sin through their response to the world. But in their reborn, perfect state they are no longer attracted to, neither do they fall prey to the subtle death plan inherent in all sensual experiences. Whereas the incorrigible egotist collects his vile animal nature from fun, excitement and adventure (with temptation), wherein lies the destiny of death, we derive our identity from the Light, who is the inner ground of our being.

The more you yearn for the truth, the less vital are material things and exciting experiences. Consequently, the more aware you become, the more you are protected from the treachery and the madness which come out of being involved. As you respond patiently to the tease and torment of the world, your new awareness protects you from reacting and taking upon yourself that karma. You can perceive subtle manipulations and dangers. While others, like lemmings, plunge over cliffs because they think they can fly or they think a more beautiful destiny awaits them, you are quietly altering your course.

Your conscience instructs you wordlessly not to go through certain doors, or it inhibits you from rushing in in an untimely way. Yet when your conscience doesn't protest, when the timing is just right, the door opens gently to health, happiness and safety. You are where you belong, prospering. Things become the extension of you; you cease to be the extension of things. You are no longer a slave.

Without true faith to inspire your life and light your way, you *must* be excited by risk and challenge. Wrong doors, troubles and excitements become terribly attractive. The exciting element of risk and the seeming possibility of change and gain beckon you toward that elusive prize. Little do you realize that you are "taking a chance" on a game that the house always wins.

Patience, on the other hand, is the discipline of your faith. It is a response, but not to temptation. Patience is the evidence that you recognize that God's laws of cause and effect are consistent; it is the sign that you wish to conform to His pattern and purpose rather than gambling on having your own willful way.

Have you ever wanted something so much that you overlooked all the things that were wrong with it? The majority of people never get beyond their impatience, their insatiable craving for people, places and things. They become more and more sensuous and guilty as

246

they get progressively entangled in the spider web of excitement and intrigue.

The journey often begins as a selfish desire is touched and awakened which sets aside conscience and allows mischief to enter. A death-oriented self emerges and grows dependent on what sustains it in its sensuality. Emotional excitement is what keeps the soul in a psychotic state. Fearful of the light, it keeps reaching for forbidden things and trying to escape the guilt of it.

Marriage tends to be one of those debilitating sensuous adventures. You see your partner one way on one side of the threshold, and another way the morning after the night before. Bored or enslaved, you then escape to someone or something else, seeking happiness: another woman, a bottle, drugs, or a new sailboat, perhaps. Any exciting thing to lose yourself in will do.

The emerging conscience threatens the evolving animal self. The light of understanding tends to tear down the identity which is not of God, as indeed it should if we are to have an imperishable character from the ground of His blessed being so that we will exist to worship and serve Him.

Now and then you read an account of a stubborn old goat who goes up in flames rather than leave his house, because he *is* his house. His house is all he has and is. The thought of facing life without his material, psychotic security is more than his ego can bear. While a house can provide security, it can also become a tyrant, because everything which comforts you owns you. Once you do business with the Mafia, for example, they own you. Government is a square Mafia; it, too, owns, exploits and eventually ruins the people through their need for its services.

Sad to say, a man will usually give up his life to his house or to his country before he will give up the foundation of pride and bare his soul to the truth. Can you see more clearly now how the infernal-eternal ego life is involved with people, places and things? As long as the sinner clings to the possessions which seem to serve him, he remains falsely secure in Satan's ancient promise. In our desperation and willfulness, we force people, places and things to serve us and make us feel secure as we falter through life.

Perhaps you have read accounts in the newspaper like that of the little child who falls into a river trying to save a toy boat to which has been attached too much importance. But another, more enlightened child shrinks back and lets the boat float away, out of reach, down the stream. The blessed child is safe! One child is growing under the law of "chance," the other under the law of perception. Perhaps the child who reaches and falls is lucky this time, and does not drown. But sooner or later, as he becomes more and more unwise through his lack of perception, his "luck" will run out and the demon of chance will have him! And there are a million different ways in which it could happen.

What you need and cling to, and what caters to you in this life, you also make your murderer. If you don't love the truth, then everything you do is bringing about your demise.

Possessing possesses you. It exerts a magical seductive influence over your mind. Possessing can make the hopeless hopeful, the impossible dream seem possible, the unbearable bearable. The power of hell can make the path to death seem like a colorful and exciting way of life.

Nevertheless, it is what it is—the final payment for the sin of pride.

If mankind were to see what death means in terms of payment for sin, they would be forced to see what is wrong with their way of life. But like the child with the toy boat, most of them will reach too far and hold on too long.

For the incorrigible egotists, the flaw of disbelief is irreversible. Doubt (which is a plague to normal men) is their passport to life. Doubt is an upside-down faith—you disbelieve the truth and believe in the lie. Prideful personalities resent being shown the folly of pride. Stubborn and incurable, they prefer to remain in sin's psychotic stupor, clutching their teddy bears of delusion and clinging to one another like a bunch of frightened monkeys. This spiritual blindness excites the wicked shepherd to close in for the kill. Licking his chops with glee, he rises from hell to serve up those exotic delights of pleasure and pain which every sinner needs, fattening them like turkeys for the feast.

Just think of it—psychotics actually enjoy being degraded by pleasant and unpleasant evils. It is impossible for them to realize that they are being exploited. They think of their psychosis-inducing experiences as fun and games, happiness, life and adventure!

Remember the sobering truth: whatever serves you becomes your lord. Crooks have their Mafia and law-abiding citizens have their government.

Pain is a warning that something is wrong, whether it is pain in the body or in society. But do psychotics heed the warning pains emanating from their insecurity? No— they simply reach for pain-killers (conscience-killers)— some new distractions to love or to hate. Whether he is respectable under the law or not, each prideful person loses his freedom to the tyranny of the emerging aristocracy of political tyrants and underworld exploiters.

There is no way out for such "victims." The choice, it seems, is between the devil and the deep sea. Escape for all who hate truth is limited to embracing error so as not to see what folly they have brought upon themselves. Their only "hope" is from their music, drugs, culture and possessions.

To buy a car because it is wise is different than buying a new car for a moral lift, to restore your faith in yourself and renew your spirit with a feeling of security. One way you are driving the car; the other way, the car is driving you. When the fender is dented, so is your reality shattered. Your relationship with your car, and other similar relationships, are a subtle form of dictatorship. No matter what it is, things addict you and become a source of frustration, both for having and not having. But you keep striving to achieve and then throwing your ill-gotten gains away until you are disillusioned and broken (if not broke). Each wrong experience with things mortifies you—it leaves you less of a human being and more of a "thing" yourself.

Anything employed as a crutch has power to destroy the real you and recreate another "you" that craves what cannot satisfy.

Have you noticed how painful and difficult it is to speak up to the friend whom you have elevated to support your ego? Your "friends" are those hypnotic crutches you need for your sinning, escaping self; their fascinating presence fulfills you by distracting your attention. To those friend/fiends goes power to hold you in the exquisite agony of a psychotic state, away from the light—free in one sense, but enslaved in another. Soon the friends seem to change and they emerge as the enemies they really were all along. Here the intrigue and the shock set you up for the psychosis of hate.

"Friends" don't really need to use overt pressure to get their way. Turning cold and unfriendly and withdrawing their support has the effect of freeing you from the false security of psychosis, allowing you to experience the pain of reality. You experience that reality as a dying. Your soul is bared, you are naked in the light. You see things clearly as they are, and yourself as you are. The agony is excruciating. The pain you feel as your guilt catches up with you will move you to do anything to get the "friend" to restore the warmth of the old relationship.

So it comes to pass that people become addicted to cruel Hitlers and "sweet Hitlers." The security provided by a cruel or "loving" presence keeps breaking down to reveal the greater evil which entered. Just as there is a tyranny of pleasure and friendship, so is there one that is centered around hate.

It is possible to be so resentful that you literally become what you hate. A man can become his mother, as in the case of a homosexual; a Jew can even become a Nazi (some of the Nazi's dirty work in the concentration camps, for example, was carried out by the Jewish *kapos*).

Tradition-addicted Jewish people were trapped in the holocaust. At first they couldn't believe the truth about what was happening to their lives. They coped with the problem in the traditional psychotic way, by denying the reality of it. Clinging to their culture, they told themselves they would be all right. They had "faith." That only excited the wicked Nazis to become more cruel. But the victims kept convincing themselves that everything would be all right. They could not believe what was happening to them. They could not stop clinging to their way of life, nor could they resist the temptation to hate wrong in order to feel right.

Another tribulation is coming, this time upon the entire world. Already, those who see the storm clouds gathering are making ready their escape, while others see only a rosy future. They may give up their lives, but never their things. The only life there is for an egotist revolves around his things, his achievements and especially his imagination, wherein he thinks lies the power to make a better world.

Evil comes into existence and thrives on that sort of blindness. If a person can't (or won't) see danger, who then can save him? Can you see that by not facing reality you are actually trying to *save yourself, to preserve your ego life?*

You will never be mugged, you will never be hurt or sick if you are truly aware. Perception will lead you out of harm's way.

Criminal psychopaths scan the passerby. The easy mark excites the parasites to close in for the kill. They know who belongs to them. And the psychotic victim is unconsciously asking for trouble. He *needs* to be exploited and degraded. Something sick in him craves this sustaining deception in all his relationships.

It is an irrevocable law that awards the unrepentant sinner's soul over to death. Get your excitement, and pay the piper! And most everyone has his own private evil shepherd who tortures, punishes and even murders him in the end. Need a doctor, anyone? To be saved by medicine is to go to the grave on the installment plan! The law is this: what saves you also claims you, so you had better be careful about what salvation you choose. Doctors don't disturb egos; they seduce them.

Home is the microcosm of the social/political macrocosm. Men who use their wives and children to support their egos are unable to stand up to them. Eventually, such men find themselves outclassed and outmaneuvered, and the whole family ends up wallowing in intrigue. Then they may rise up in violent rebellion against their family or government, but nothing positive can come of that either.

Hating wrong as a way of feeling right is not the same as loving right. Wait too long to nip wrong in the bud, and you will cultivate violence and tyranny. Why don't you stand up for what is right, then? Because you have a secret need for the wrongs you are tolerating and cultivating. You need to hate someone to stay secure in your self-righteousness.

Both angry rebellion and submission give power to the mugger, the racist, the tyrant husband, wife, boss or dictator. Even a democratic form of government eventually becomes a jailer to the people when they elect leaders to it who will keep them secure in their selfish prejudice.

Happily, it *is* possible to obtain the potential benefits from marriage and from a democratic form of government, but only if the people are awake.

Unaware, psychotics are weak counterparts of their wicked overlords, unconsciously bound to elect tyrants in one form or another. Sinners are not free to elect godly men. Cannibals elect cannibal kings, don't they? And through the inherent influence of cannibal kings, cannibals can never hope to be anything except better cannibals. Like cannibals, hypocrites keep electing dishonest politicians to tell them what they want to hear.

Generally, the masses have little tolerance for honesty. People elect governments for the same reasons the fool buys a new car or gets married—not out of wisdom and love, but out of foolish need.

The effects of doing those things for those different reasons are opposite. One way leads toward greater freedom, happiness, and an unfolding heavenly order in your home and throughout the land. The other way leads to chaos, bondage and cataclysm through tyranny, which takes many different forms. There is the tyranny of alcohol, drugs, material things, medicine, music, husbands, wives, churches, labor—and last, but perhaps worst of all, the tyranny of political dictatorship.

Although they themselves are responsible for bringing into existence the counter-culture, the heads of state are naturally envious of its role in illegally assisting the people's psychosis. Like jealous women, the aristocracy of elected officials fear losing their power to the various criminal sub-culture dictatorships. And they all fight over the miserable carcasses of the people, like a mother and daughter-in-law fighting over the wretched son.

Like the underworld creeps they mostly are, government officials never address themselves to the real cause of social problems for fear the people will awaken to their addiction to culture and its puppet bureaucracies of business, religion and medicine which parasite on their weakness.

The sleepwalking serfs in democratic feudal systems

254

are caught between the parasites of the underworld and the cultural barons. Between them, they perpetuate the social and the anti-social systems, both of which encourage the weakness of the people, who are lined up at the trough like cows—so busy feeding their egos that they don't know they are being milked. The dictatorship of this kind of liberty sets us up for the ultimate dictatorship of chains. The kind of people who teach you to abuse freedom are quietly busy building cages.

Those who belong to either the bureaucratic or the criminal hierarchy have a rich way of living; their psychotic victims have an expensive way of dying, which *seems* like living. The psychopaths are the kings and queens of culture, the creators of the psychotics' dreamworld, and the payment for their services is death.

The payment for sin has always been death. But without truth to reveal death for what it is, we can turn it around to mean something natural and noble. Sleepwalking, the world is headed for destruction. Only those few who can see the handwriting on the wall will make provisions and be saved.

After a lifetime of corruption, too afraid to face the truth, the old can come to see death as a blessing. Death is the scoundrel's last refuge from reality; it is the last and ultimate psychotic episode. Everything is backwards in this world—death is life, hell is heaven, and darkness is light. Evil is "live" spelled backwards.

Your sin life depends upon evil inspiring your ego with a sense of well-being. You use evil by loving it and being loved in return, and you use it again when you hate and are hated.

You award a good judgment to the sustaining evil for

serving your kingly feelings. Later you hate it for betraying you. Between these two extreme emotions, your ego is held fixated away from reality in a psychotic state of judgment. The psychotic always winds up with the booby prize—he gets to sit on an imaginary throne as king and judge.

As a psychotic, your entire life is sustained by the use of something evil or the abuse of something intended for your good. A typical male, for example, must either have an outright whore, or make his wife serve the same purpose—a helpmate is not enough for him.

The lower you sink, the more you need the services of evil to help you stay ahead of the judgment you feel on yourself. Any way you slice it, it is always wickedness which sustains you in your delusions of grandeur and self-righteousness. Your ego development is entrusted to Satan through human agencies.

Foolish souls love to love evil, and my, how they love to hate it!

As I said before, when you deal with the Mafia, they own you. They have an unwritten spiritual law on their side that allows hell to claim what rightfully belongs to it.

As they say, "everything is relative"—if the Creator isn't your relative, then Satan is! Therefore, take heed!

Don't use people, and they won't become your masters.

All addiction is enslavement to an ego support. *Addiction represents the stubbornness of pride escaping reality.* When you reject reality, all you have left is the supporting agent. As you drink it in, it will drink in you. Even as you ache for it, you vomit in your need. The female you degrade for your pleasure will suck the vitality out of your body!

Psychopaths take great pleasure in torturing their

victims, inflicting upon them the greatest possible amount of punishment and pain. But psychopaths are still people—whom psychotics have converted to the wretched role of eating them alive. *By electing them to serve your ego, you have made them your executioners.* You have made them twice as ripe for hell as you are yourself. They have this loathing, this contempt for you because you have drawn up through them the Dracula spirit who delights in the hellish eternal life derived from drinking your blood. They suffer the ambivalence of reveling in, yet loathing, their role of part demon, part man!

Hell's aristocracy suffer the tortures of the damned simply because you, their psychotic victims, have helped them to attain infernal eternal power which requires the exquisite agony of murder (yours) to maintain it. But they are merely jailers manacled to their wretched prisoners, closer to the reality of hell than the "victims" who raised them from the pit of iniquity. The masses have raised up hell as if it were heaven and death as life, because their souls love deception, not truth.

Emotional "blood" is the psychopath's life, yet it burns inside him because of the sin. How sweet is the contempt! And God, how it burns! Is there nowhere one who will free him from his agony through the blood of Christ's love?

Gentlemen, do you realize now why your wives have this kind of contempt for you? Have you not set them up to support your selfishness and you delusions of manhood? Little wonder that many women get away with murder.

There is no hell greater than a woman's scorn. She suffers the ecstasy and agony of the male's dying to her as he gives her sex-life instead of love-life. Yet her contempt only frightens the male into a deeper psychotic state of rage or sexual submission, while she goes mad with power and frustration.

God does not make us suffer. It is our sinfulness, our weakness, that draws oppression out of the pit. People suffer because they are always tricked into suffering, choosing evil as though it were good. *People suffer because they deserve to suffer. Our Creator does not make our lives bitter, wretched and miserable. We bring it all upon ourselves.*

Let me remind you again that the term psychotic is a psychological pseudonym for sinner or slave. Re-read this chapter over and over and your eyes will open to see its deeper meaning. The Bible tells us that all who sin are slaves, and that the wages of sin is death.

Remember, there are two ways of looking at everything. It is the manner in which the experience or object invites or is used that causes it to become exciting to the psychotic. A female body is exciting only to the degree that it invites the male to look upon it in that certain way. Women know when men are looking like that and are quick to take advantage.

Any object you care to think of, and even those you don't, can affect you in the same way a woman's body can. If it doesn't tease you, you can do something in your mind to make it tease. Sex becomes lust and lust becomes synonymous with life; it is the same with avarice and gluttony. It seems only natural to want to own those things that make you feel secure—but they always end by possessing you, and that is the bottom line.

We become old, diseased and we die because we run

out of energy. For mankind there are two ways to use vitality:

1) to build a prideful animal-self, or
2) to build an eternal life-self.

You need every ounce of life force to make the change from mortality to immortality. Alas, you dissipate your vital force pursuing the "life" of pride.

You must be like the caterpillar undergoing metamorphosis to become a butterfly. You are designed to transcend the pride and the mortal nature. This can occur only if you lay down your psychotic ego-animal life, a life based on sensual experiences with people, places and things. At any moment you can awaken to realize, like that child with the toy boat, that the "boat" is not everything. Which child will you be? The one who holds on too long and drowns, or the other?

Most of us are the sum total of our experiences, but another way of saying this is that we are burdened down and bothered by our past. Unless we learn to respond properly in the present moment, the present becomes merely an extension of that burdensome past.

Roy Masters, author of this persuasive self-help book, describes a remarkably simple technique to help us face life properly, calmly. He shows us that it is the way we respond emotionally to pressures that makes us sick and depressed.

By leading us back to our center of dignity and understanding and showing us how to apply one simple principle, Roy Masters shows us how to remain sane, poised and tranquil under the most severe trials and tribulations.

Roy Masters has nothing less to offer you than the secret of life itself—how to get close to yourself and find your lost identity, the true self you have lost in the confusion.

The observation exercise materials consist of the book, *How Your Mind Can Keep You Well,* and three (3) cassettes of the same title. We suggest a donation of $30, or whatever you can afford.